BARRY

Tony Jasper has been a contemporary music author and broadcaster for many years. He is a past Charts Editor of *Record Mirror* and feature writer for *Easy Listening*. He writes weekly for *The Manchester Evening News*, reviews weekly for Europe's leading music industry trade paper *Music Week* and has radio programmes for Radio Hallam and BFBS. Past books have included studies of Rod Stewart, Paul McCartney, Elton John, The Rolling Stones and Cliff Richard. His record chart and factual books *The British Record Charts* and *The 70s – A Book Of Records* have gained him a strong reputation. He was born in Penzance and now lives in London.

BARRY MANILOW

Tony Jasper

A STAR BOOK
published by
the Paperback Division of
W. H. ALLEN & Co. Ltd

A Star Book
Published in 1981
by the Paperback Division of
W. H. Allen & Co. Ltd
A Howard and Wyndham Company
44 Hill Street, London W1X 8LB

Copyright © Tony Jasper 1981

Typeset by
Computacomp (UK) Ltd, Fort William,
Scotland

Printed in Great Britain by
Hunt Barnard Printing Ltd., Aylesbury, Bucks.

ISBN 0 352 31002 2

This book is sold subject to the condition that
it shall not, by way of trade or otherwise, be
lent, re-sold, hired out or otherwise
circulated without the publisher's prior
consent in any form of binding or cover
other than that in which it is published and
without a similar condition including this
condition being imposed on the subsequent
purchaser.

CONTENTS

To
Mollie and Lynn for their support and time in compiling
this book.

To
Ed and Betty Armstrong for years of friendship.

Very special thanks to Mollie and Lynn of the British Barry Manilow Fan Club, Howard Harding, Annie Ivel, numerous BMFC members, Sue Richardson, Adam White and the many people who offered information and advice while I was compiling this book.

INTRODUCTION

As a journalist I am fascinated by how someone like Barry Manilow with all the early odds against him nevertheless wins through.

His is the story of self-belief, talent and at the right time a shrewdness which in its major application has meant his choosing the right people to guide the many aspects of his career.

This is the story of a current superstar. There are many who do not like his voice and who equally dislike his songs. What they cannot deny is his multi-million album and single sales, the ability to sell out a concert within an hour of the box office opening. His supporters well out-number the detractors.

I have found there is universal praise for Barry as a person, as a musician, arranger and producer, and not merely his best known forte of singing and writing hit songs. I have found Barry a charming person.

Writing this story of Barry Manilow has made me realise there is a larger musical world than merely rock.

BEFORE THE BIG TIME

New York is the city which never sleeps. It's a constant buzz of frenetic activity even when the temperature soars past the 95° F mark or conversely descends down into the body chilling regions of minus 15° F.

New York is the focal point of the northeastern part of the United States and with the United Nations headquarters within its perimeters some would say the city is the world's political capital.

It's a cosmopolitan city, it houses and gives temporary residence to a miriad of races; it gives publishing, advertising, finance and entertainment a market place; it boasts streets of high fashion and shopping centres which sell the produce of the world with due understatement as if the goods came from but half-a-mile away.

Brooklyn, one of New York's suburbs, is an area full of churches. It has half-a-dozen parks, an assortment of higher learning institutions, the 500-acre Prospect Park, a famous museum, and an equally respected Botanic Garden, not to mention the famed Coney Island.

Coney Island faces the Atlantic. In time gone by it saw itself as a fashionable beach resort. In recent times it has become known as the mecca for fairground amusement lovers.

Another Brooklyn landmark is the monumental Grand

Army Plaza with its 80-foot high memorial arch. There is also the Italianate villa, built in 1857 and once the home of Edward C. Litchfield, a railway pioneer, which has been described as one of the most elegant domestic buildings of its time.

Brooklyn boasts the New York Aquarium where at feeding time an electric eel suitably tickled by an attendant emits some 650 volts. The Sheepshead Bay area is a mini-port for saltwater fishermen. Old city relics can be found in the Sculpture Garden.

This New York borough is home to a mixture of races. In historical times it was populated by Carnarsie Indians, then came the Normans, the French and English colonists from Massachusetts. Its street names tell of times when feuds between differing peoples were common. Brooklyn Heights affords a marvellous view of Manhattan while the older homes contrast starkly with the not-too-distant contemporary sky-scrapers of central New York. Abraham Lincoln's historic speech against slavery was made at the Cooper Institute for it was an area where the Abolitionist movement flourished in the nineteenth century.

So the young Barry Manilow grew up in an historic area. It is known for its endless variety and colour but, like New York boroughs as a whole, comparative poverty is always but a street away from affluence.

Barry was born on 17 June 1946 in the Williamsburg section of Brooklyn. He was not from a financially well-off background. His father left home when he was a mere two-year-old and he was brought up by a devoted mother and grandparents. His mother was twenty when his father left.

The young Barry has been described as a scrawny kid with a prominent nose, buck teeth and blond hair. His grandfather was Joe Manilow. Barry remembers that he was taken to Times Square when he was two years old and there he operated a make-a-record machine and was told to sing 'Happy Birthday'. This recording of a handful of syllables can now be found on the *Barry Manilow II* album.

People said he would be a singer even before he sang a proper controlled note. He liked the Andrews Sisters when he was three and he heard rock 'n' roll music at the candy store as people fed the juke-box. At seven he was having accordion lessons, by thirteen he was learning the piano and he was taken to hear prominent jazz musicians of the time.

Barry was taught a Jewish version of the Protestant work ethic: times and conditions were hard and any improvement in living standards could only come from hard work. It stood him well in the musical field, the simple truth that success comes from endless practice and constant striving for the highest of standards. And that often means that the normal pleasures of life have to take a back seat.

It seems that in that hard neighbourhood the young Barry often got beaten up by tougher and bigger boys and was often ridiculed for the nose and for his lack of flesh. Now he has the last laugh, for unlike some of his contemporaries he fought his way out of a comparative slum to the bright lights beyond. Some writers call it a modern Cinderella story.

Barry says he told the kids of his youth that one day he would be a star. He says they were merely amused and some were even downright spiteful. They played in the street and he practised his accordion. For all that Barry was not a brooding kid, shut away from the world, he missed his father dearly and something of this can be caught in the song 'Ships That Pass In The Night'.

He began smoking when he was nine but had given it up at the great age of fifteen! Later he took up the habit once more but gave it up soon after. He dispensed with the habit because he felt it would interfere with the demands of the show-biz life he had set his sights upon.

His mom was like a sister. Barry says: 'My grandparents raised her and me at the same time. It was more like having a sister than a mother. It was an interesting way of being raised. They'd tell both of us to go to sleep; we were up too late.' His father was a truckdriver. He suddenly turned up in 1976 at a concert Barry was giving in New York. 'I know it sounds cold but I don't know him. It's too emotional for me to go into detail.'

His mother re-married in Barry's bar mitzvah year. Her new husband, Willie Murphy, was a jazz freak.

'Nobody told me there was jazz or show music out there. But the first thing Willie Murphy did was to take me to a Gerry Mulligan concert. I'll never forget it. It was the biggest thing in my life.' The teenage Barry heard the Beatles and adored Barbra Streisand. When he heard the Jewish lady he felt here was the perfect example of all musical elements coming together, with songwriter, producer, musical arranger, accompanist, recording and vocalist combining to produce contemporary music of the highest quality.

Money was scarce for the youthful Barry. He took courses in advertising in New York City College but he soon turned his thoughts toward the world he loved – music. He signed up at the New York College of Music and the Julliard School. The advertising course had concerned itself with the marketing and merchandising of textiles. It was interesting but it didn't really spark his enthusiasm.

He spent two semesters at the Julliard School of Music. He says: 'I told myself, aw, come on an' give music a try.' Well, it was what he always wanted!

Rock 'n' Roll made no early impression upon Barry and he says 'Rock Around The Clock', Bill Haley's multimillion world hit, was hardly his favourite. His liking for rock increased after the Beatles had found amazing success in the United States. Apart from Barbra he also admired another stunning lady from New York's Bronx area, Laura Nyro. She lived on College Avenue. Her dad was a trumpeter and she began songwriting at the age of eight. She attended the High School of Music and Art in Manhattan.

In her late teens Laura meddled with drugs and in one acid trip experienced a harrowing journey of the mind in which half-men, half-rat monsters stormed her room in an attempt to kill her. This terrifying episode she has described as the turning point in her life. Her songwriting activities increased and though she was jeered off stage at the famous 1967 Monterey Pop Festival it did mean her songs were heard by musicians. These last were more discerning than the fans who found the constant awkward composition of her songs sometimes beyond their comprehension. The songs, as far as they were concerned, were not improved by Laura Nyro, the vocalist, who sang with a penetrating thinnish-sounding tone. Early in 1968 her first album was released by US Columbia (CBS in the UK): *Eli And The Thirteenth Confession*. Music critics heralded a major new talent. Barry Manilow, just one year younger than Laura and at that time a songwriter, was in the company of those who rightfully saw a new star in the making.

Streisand was of course from Barry's home territory. She was born in 1942 in Brooklyn. Hit albums with a million sales apiece had regularly come for the lady from her early twenties. She was everything that the later Barry would become, an acknowledged superstar, brilliant in a number of media. Barry has yet to make an impact in the world of films, but Manilow's supporters say this is a field he will almost certainly conquer.

Barry's musical college training was in part financed by a job in the mailroom of CBS records. And, of course, this work within the confines of America's major record company brought him into contact with or at least the proximity of the men who sign, record and further the careers of the record stars. CBS had in the late 1950s enjoyed amazing sales from records by stars such as Frankie Laine, Johnny Ray, Guy Mitchell, Doris Day and arranger and producer Mitch Miller plus his orchestra. CBS had entered the 1960s with high-selling acts like Tony Bennett, Paul & Paula, Percy Faith, Johnny Mathis and within a few years Johnny Cash.

By now Barry had left home and had married his childhood sweetheart Susan. He took a room in fashionable and trendy Greenwich Village. He played at bar mitzvahs and weddings and with a jazz band which played in the bars until three or so in the morning. The Greenwich Village flat, like his home in Brooklyn, was a far cry from his present home in California. His Californian house was built in the 1950s, and its grounds cover over two-and-a-half acres. He can see over the mountains in Bel Air.

'I never thought I'd say this but I'm not comfortable in New York any more. I don't know what to make of it, it's my home town. The craziness, the insane energy, the dirt, it makes me nervous.

'When I first moved to Los Angeles I used to say: "You can get a pizza in New York at 3 a.m. and you can't here." Then I realised that I'd never actually felt the desire for one. Now, in California, I've created a lifestyle which is paradise, the air is clean and I'm gonna stay here.'

This is what he was to say in November 1980 but back in the mid-1960s it was different. New York was America's recording capital, the music scene had not migrated west. The recording studios had not yet made the move to California and life in New York was exciting.

His marriage to Susan, whose maiden name has never been disclosed, lasted but a year. 'I was too young, I had not discovered the fact that all I wanted was music.'

Meanwhile his musical career prospered.

His idea of taking a job in the CBS mailroom bore fruit. His musical talent became known. He met Linda Allen. Later she was to become his general manager and ever-present companion. They now share an apartment and have done so for twelve years. In 1981, Barry said: 'My mother is always saying I should get married. I guess she wants grandchildren.'

Linda worked in the programme department at CBS. She gave him the opportunity of arranging the music of the new late show for a local TV station.

Barry, then just eighteen years old, followed this with some arranging for a CBS musical director and went on to work on a musical entitled *The Drunkard*. Here he re-arranged non-copyright songs but he also wrote some new material. *The Drunkard* ran both on and off Broadway for a total of eight years. The show's popularity was in part due to Barry's music. It made his name known and it gained for him a growing respect.

In 1967 he directed a WCBS-TV talent series *Callback*. Then he conducted and arranged for the famous US presenter, Ed Sullivan, and for various TV shows and assignments.

Everything was happening for Barry and like anyone who finds he is becoming popular on all sides he began to be faced with the necessity of making important decisions about his future. He had written music for three off-Broadway musicals and he was offered the job of going on the road with one of them. He had problems in making up his mind. Barry tried to envisage what might happen if he accepted the job. He considered the direst of consequences. He might return and find that he had no job. That would mean another uphill struggle to establish a new base.

He told Sue Reid of the *Sunday Telegraph Magazine*: 'I had a promising career as a junior executive. I'd created all my childhood fantasies of becoming a businessman, put all the pieces together, and it felt wrong. I was in such a turmoil that, without telling my wife, I wrote to the advice column of *Playboy* asking for help.'

His letter was published and these days it hangs on the wall of his office. The letter written in December 1967 read:

Music has always been a vital part of my life. Due to financial difficulties, however, I had to stop attending music school and accept a job at a leading radio and television network. Through enormous good fortune, I have been promoted very rapidly, and at the age of 22 I hold a junior executive position with a very generous salary. The only drawback is that this position has absolutely nothing to do with music.

During these past few years, between working and attending college, I have managed to musically direct and conduct three full-scale musicals at various theatre workshops in New York. I now have an offer to take this last musical out of town for a period of six to eight months at a good salary with the promise of a permanent position as a musical director.

My musical wild oats are screaming to be sown, but it means giving up my secure job. Leaves of absence are rare, so it looks like it's one or the other. Any suggestions? B.M., Brooklyn, New York.

He received a reply from *Playboy*:

Follow your real interest and take the musical out of town. At your age, your financial responsibilities are few. If you remain in the secure job, you may regret it for the rest of your life that you didn't sow your oats. You can always go back to radio and television: your ability was recognised once; chances are it would be recognised again – if not with your former employer, then elsewhere.

Surprisingly it might seem, Barry, at first, decided not to take their advice. He rowed with his wife and they parted. He then went and saw his boss at CBS.

The meeting went well, very well. He left with an assurance from his boss that he could have his job back when he returned. So off he went with another important turn in his career under way. And now he was single once more.

'I felt tied down and believed there must be more in life than coming home and watching television. Susan became a hippy and went to San Francisco. We still meet now and again. I try and block out of my mind the day I walked out on her.' And so the non-drinker, non-car owner Barry pushed his frontiers forward. There was now no stopping him.

During this period he also met Lee Gurst. Gurst was in New York for the purposes of attending college. He had been hired to work on *New*, an off-Broadway show which had Barry as its musical director. Barry also played piano. Gurst was on drums. The two saw eye-to-eye and so began a long musical acquaintance.

He was busily coaching, composing and playing for other singers. He became interested in writing commercials. At one time in 1967 he was writing and arranging sixteen songs a week for the already mentioned *Callback* series. He later had his own act with a girl singer which was headlined as Jeannie and Barry. One of those who met him toward the end of the 1960s was an aspiring singer and actress called Lynette Bennett.

FIRST IMPRESSIONS ARE GOOD

Hot New York summer days are no one's friend. On one such occasion toward the end of the 1960s Lynette Bennett made her way to the courtyard of Christ Church, Park Avenue and 60th Street. She was feeling the heat. Romance was far from her mind. Little did she realise that the man who would win her heart was innocently making his way toward the same direction. He was a young theological student by the name of Warren Danskin. Lynette had designs on a theatrical career and was busily polishing up her singing. She had thoughts of making a record and, who knows, even emulating Barbra Streisand. Lynette knew people rated her work highly. Suddenly there he was — Warren Danskin. It was heart-flutter time. Their eyes met. They spoke. They made their way to the Church restaurant. Their time was short, for Lynette had an appointment with an up-and-coming arranger and accompanist. Lynette excused herself and said she must go and phone this man. Warren was told not to worry.

Lynette's mystery man was called Barry Manilow! Barry had been working with her flatmate and she had assured Lynette that Barry would be just the right person to further her musical career and to lend aid for a demo record which she was planning. So she phoned Barry in

Brooklyn. He said he would come to her flat on Central Park West. Later the meetings were at his flat for Barry had an eight-track on which they could dub her songs. They were happy times, endless hours singing, playing and discussing. Lynette recognised Barry's utter musical dedication and his complete desire for perfection. She also saw the talent which was awaiting full bloom. Years later, in the summer of 1981, she left London for New York after seven years living in Britain's capital city. She departed with husband Warren who had been for this period of time Minister of the American Church in Tottenham Court Road. In the period from the late 1960s to the early 1980s Lynette had developed her own successful career as a singer and actress. Toward the end of the 1970s she auditioned successfully for a major role in the hit musical *Chicago*, and starred in the West End until the show closed in 1980. She appeared under the name of Lynette Bentley for there is and was already a Lynette Bennett in the UK.

Before she left London she talked with me in a flat which was just a street away from the American Embassy. Lynette is tall. She walks gracefully, is glamorous, her manner and general aplomb befits a star. Barry has never left her thoughts. She is a Manilow fan. She adores his music, his performance, his show-biz persona. She takes quiet satisfaction in the fact that she sang and played with Barry back in his formative days. She feels he has not changed as a person in spite of the incredible world acclaim which has come his way over the years.

'I remember my first impression of him. He was so sweet. He had a nice style in singing and playing. The period of our meeting was when hard rock was flourishing but his style was gentle rock.' The two talked music and little else. Lynette remembers her curiosity over what other interests he might possess.

'I just didn't find any. I don't remember any pet

passion of his. I suppose he had some but I don't remember things that strong. He was just into music.

'Sometimes we would encounter a problem in the music. We would then go for a walk in the park. I remember the night before we were due to record a demo. He rang and he said he wondered whether I was prepared. I found that tremendous. I mean I was paying him as the accompanist. He said we must wait, we needed one more rehearsal. He really cared, it wasn't just money which dictated what he did – far from it.

'Barry would always talk things through. He was good for things like that. As it happened the demo session turned out nicely. That guy is gifted. He's creative. And he's such a nice guy. He really is.'

Lynette says she particularly admires how Barry fought his way out of poverty and the obvious sacrifices he made on the way. Not that this means she is always and forever approving of whatever Barry does.

'I heard him a few years later. I suppose it may have been around 1975 or so and he was playing loudly and I thought this is not Barry at his best. I think I and others love the gentle Barry. Still I heard him again and then I thought he's now got a good director, the act is better focused and choreographed, everything was better staged and the whole thing was more of a production.

'I think Barry is a natural actor and the acting approach to a song is shining through beautifully now and in a stronger way than it used to.'

She remembers how she marvelled at his determination and says: 'He grew up as a street kid, he did a lot of self-teaching. I liked him very much. We were chummy, good friends! He's such a wholesome person and to think that someone like that can make it in show-business is very pleasing.'

And there was the pleasant occasion when Barry told her, 'I look forward to coming up here,' as he spoke of his visits. At this time in his career money came in spasmodic dribs and drabs. Lynette calls it a time: 'When you eat you do it well, and when you do not, well …'

Lynette with Barry as accompanist recorded four vocal tracks for a version of a Donovan song, 'Wear Your Love Like Heaven' and a first take was enough each time, such was the thorough work which the two had done. They recorded two other songs for the demo. It was duly taken by Lynette to RCA record in New York. She went with high hopes. 'I wore a mini-skirt, I remember. It was fashionable then but I was straight looking.' It was a dress which appealed to the gentleman at RCA. He said it clearly told him the kind of demo she had brought and it was not the sound he was looking for. It was a sad occasion but now looking back at the event she is amused. 'I would like to meet up with him again and say, "Hey, you missed Barry Manilow!" Barry, of course, wasn't singing at the time, he was playing the piano and acting as musical director and he had written the arrangements.'

Naturally Lynette went and heard Barry perform. One location was the Upstairs at the Downstairs Club where Barry was the opening act in a billing which had writer turned comedian Joan Rivers as the star turn.

She remembers sitting there with a smile on her face. 'Whatever Barry did was carefully presented and it was tasteful.' She recalls being with Barry on one occasion when he busily taught Lee Gurst the bossa nova beat. And there is memory of Barry exquisitely arranging 'Laia La Dia' for her, as a dance routine for her cabaret act.

'He was really excited doing that, wanting the drums and cymbals to catch the kicks from the girls. He hadn't written dance music before.'

Lynette herself at this period of time, at the end of the 1960s, had been in several Broadway productions and had a very promising career ahead. Meeting Barry and hiring him as accompanist taught her a great deal.

'Barry wasn't in love with me,' she says with a smile. And she herself was in love with Warren. Barry had been in her mind on the day she met Warren. And he was very much part of the day when she and Warren became engaged!

'Well, Warren had proposed and I had accepted. There we were newly engaged, hand-in-hand waiting for a bus on 8th Avenue. We had told no one. And then who should we bump into but Barry. I just simply said, "Barry, this is my fiancé," simple as that. He smiled. I'll never forget the meeting. It was quite unexpected though I had talked about Barry to Warren a great deal.'

Lynette's musical partnership with Barry came to an end. She has personal memories and she has quite a bit of early Barry on tape. She finds it an amusing thought that maybe one day she can land on his doorstep clutching the rejected demo, but 'it's been a long time since', and each has found success in their way.

Inevitably the two have neither seen nor spoken to each other for many years. However in a conversation with Barry during early summer of 1981 I reminded him of Lynette and gave him her good wishes. There was a moment's pause and then a hint of recognition in the voice which grew to definite sureness. 'That was a long time back,' he said, and then went on to say how happy those days were. He sent his good wishes and obviously was thinking some more of their times together. And back in the late 1960s Lynette remembers how she heard of his increasing involvement in the writing and singing of commercials and eventually of a major landmark in his career – the time when he took the job as piano player at New York's Continental Baths where he met the legendary Bette Midler.

COMMERCIALS AND BETTE

New York, 2 March 1977, the time is 10.00 p.m. Millions of the city's inhabitants are tuned into Channel 5 to see Barry's first TV special. Penny Marshall of the Laverne and Shirley TV duo are booked for an appearance. It became one of the season's highest rated shows and was nominated for three Emmy honours.

The show has one unusual and unexpected item. It takes the viewer right back into Barry's past when he struggled for money and sought ways of finding recognition, if not fame itself.

Barry performs a commercial medley. He runs through the catchy words and rhythms of adverts for Kentucky Fried Chicken, Dr Pepper, Pepsi, Chevrolet, State Farm Insurance, Stridex, Bowlene Toilet Cleanser and Band-Aids. He wrote the last five.

For his second TV show Barry had Ernest Chambers as producer. Chambers is the gentleman who was behind the smooth running of the original Smothers Brothers show and another series which starred Tony Orlando and drew high rating figures. The show's opening sequence features Barry's mother, Edna Murphy. She is seen as a businesswoman living in Manhattan. She has a dispute with a taxi driver. The guy isn't arguing with her about the fare. It's simply the fact that he's dared suggest he has never heard of Barry Manilow! It doesn't go down at all well with Edna. She puts him right. The show features Ray Charles, Desi Arnaz Sr, sixteen show girls, children and senior citizens and some animated sequences.

Barry sang his commercials in his stage show presentation as he toured the country but there was one he never liked. The non-favourite was the McDonald's hamburger advert. He has commented: 'And if one more person gives me credit for writing that stupid McDonald's jingle, I will not be responsible for what I do with my next Big Mac!' As for commercials in general, Barry's philosophy is one he applies to a good pop song: 'In both cases you have to stick to one simple idea, and get it across as directly as possible.' It makes sense.

Barry's use of commercial numbers to form a show medley obviously set people wondering how he became involved in this industry. It seems that he wrote a song for a singer he was busily coaching. This person decided he would record the number as a demo and then take it around various agencies. This he did with some success. He was hired as a singer and the client also asked who wrote the music. As a result, Barry was asked for more material. This he supplied and valuable commissions flooded in. Later Barry sang his own commercial vocals. He drily remarked one day: 'I decided you make more money from singing commercials!' At one time he worked for five different agencies. Barry's comment on this was pragmatic and down to earth, 'It was better than playing in bars.'

By 1978 Barry was on the verge of dropping his medley routine of commercials. He had called it his 'Very Strange Medley' spot. As the hit songs accumulated and audience pressures for them all in his programme grew louder and more insistent so it became a problem to decide what to leave out of the show. This medley routine seemed an obvious choice for omission. And there were those who thought the routine commercialised the act too much.

In the late summer of 1978 when he appeared at the Pine Knob in Detroit the 'commercial spot' was ousted. There was not even one brief vocal reminder of the world which made him a tidy sum of money before he began selling his albums and singles by the million. In his previous two Detroit concerts the VSM medley was a high point. Here, on this occasion, he told the packed house: 'For four-and-a-half years I've done my commercials and this year I figured I had enough bona fide hits of my own to do a medley.' He proved his point by launching into 'Tryin' To Get The Feeling', 'Mandy', 'Could It Be Magic' 'This One's For You', 'Daybreak', 'It's A Miracle' and 'Can't Smile Without You'. The point was well and truly made. The audience loved the new sure and confident Barry. He no longer needed the past to remind people of where he had been and come from. He was a creature of the present and future. There was no more need to look over his shoulder.

Yet the commercial past had been beneficial. He had met on these dates a talented lady by the name of Melissa Manchester and once he described her as the only real pal he had in the business.

Melissa has become one of the America's finest contemporary singers with a string of hit albums and singles. Sadly her fame has never reached England.

Melissa was from the Bronx. She was born on 15 February 1951. Her father was renowned for his bassoon work with the Metropolitan Opera Orchestra. She graduated from the illustrious High School Of Performing Arts in Manhattan. When she was sixteen she joined Chappel Music as a staff writer and at the same time continued her musical studies by attending New York's University School Of The Arts. Her tutor in songwriting and production was Paul Simon.

She recorded for Bell in 1973 and was retained when

Bell became Arista. One of her major albums was *Help Is On The Way* which was released in 1977. It vividly focused on vinyl her inspiring versatility, from the fragile, crystalline beauty of the song 'Be Somebody' to the raucous energy of 'A Fool In Love'. Her major hit in the States during the '70s was 'Midnight Blue', a tender romantic ballad. The album contained more of her own songs and one was written with another popular American singer-songwriter Carole Bayer Sager. Barry had sung his way around the American radio and television network, no mean feat and not of minor significance when placed against the basic fact that the US unlike Britain has no national station. The ads had made his music and his voice familiar to millions long before the hit records came with all their sudden and immediate fury. The only slight disadvantage lay perhaps in the tiresome proneness of critics and feature writers to always preface their reviews and articles with a mention of this commercial ad activity of early times. It took some people a long time to erase from their consciousness the idea of Barry Manilow – the man who made commercials.

And the 'commercial medley' had been particularly useful when he made his first tour. At that time he had achieved no hits and so the ad spot was a most useful means of reminding people that he was the voice they heard constantly day in and day out between programmes as they watched TV. It was like starting out with hit records. The public loved them, even if some writers kept asking such questions as 'Does Barry Manilow deserve a break today?' and laughing at the ad he wrote for a toilet bowl cleaner. Barry remarked that when he looked at the write-ups in the early days 'it was like knives' but he learnt to live with the critics who were always gunning for him and to put aside the barbed comments of people who were strictly rock fans who went with Kiss and bought Led Zeppelin.

The commercial ad activity was useful but the path toward real stardom, though he did not realise this at the time, came through his engagement to accompany Bette Midler at New York's Continental Baths.

Barry remembers their first meeting with some amusement. Candidly he says: 'It was hate at first sight. Two Jews in one room not liking each other. But we rehearsed anyway, and Saturday night came and there I was at the Continental Baths in a roomful of naked men and towels and Bette came on stage looking like my mother with a fox around her neck and a turban on her head. I was rolling under the piano. I cried during the ballads and she totally knocked me for a loop.'

Bette was from Patterson, New Jersey. She was named by her mum after movie star Bette Davis. Throughout her early youth she harboured thoughts of being a great actress. After high school and the University of Hawaii she looked for a chance to break into theatre. Eventually she landed an 'extra' part in the 1965 film *Hawaii*. Later she settled in New York and mingled with theatre people. For three years she sang in the chorus of *Fiddler On The Roof* — well, with Bette nothing is that simple! In fact she wormed her way out of the chorus and into the role of Tevye, the eldest daughter of the show's main character. There was a part in the rock musical *Salvation* and she saw many major musical stars who inspired her toward that powerful ambition — real stardom. Whenever she got the chance she sang, whatever the size of the club or venue. At the same time she began taking acting lessons with Bob Elston who was one of the teachers at the Herbert Berghof studio. It was he who spoke of a friend who needed someone to entertain at the Continental Baths, an apparent favoured spot for homosexuals. She went down a bomb and gays clamoured to see and hear her. And there, on piano, was the singer-songwriter from Brooklyn, fellow Jew, Barry Manilow.

31

The year was 1972 and at first it was just a weekend engagement for Barry, but short or long it was magic : the two gelled. Stephen E. Rubin wrote in the *Chicago Tribune* of 13 February 1977, when recalling the Baths partnership:

No one will ever know for sure how much of it was Barry and how much of it was Bette, but together they had an extraordinary impact. Barry was in the background arranging material, masterminding the stage act, and co-producing her albums, while Bette let loose the torrential energy and chutzpah that became her trademarks. Although they've ceased working together, Barry speaks of 'the divine Miss M' with awe.

'I love Bette. She's my favourite entertainer. Our relationship ended fine. It just stopped.' So speaks Barry. The end came in 1973 but long after the days of the Baths had ceased Barry was Bette's arranger and accompanist on tour.

However while he played at the Baths Barry had caught the attention of various record company personnel who had initially come to catch Bette in action. One of these was Ron Dante, a talented record producer who worked for the famous Don Kirshner.

Kirshner agreed with Dante's assessment of the Manilow magic and he concurred with the suggestion that they should sign Barry for their publishing company. It never happened for the simple reason that terms were never agreed but the three have always remained friends. Barry spent three years as Bette's music director, conductor and pianist. For the New Jersey bundle of fire success came quickly. Within a short time she was billed at the famous Carnegie Hall. On New Year's Eve of 1972 she starred at New York's Philharmonic Hall in the Lincoln Centre. Late '72 Atlantic released her *The Divine Miss M* and the 100,000 sales mark was passed within weeks. Later sales hit half a million and the album was nominated for a Grammy award. The album credits had Barry listed with Ahmet Ertegun and Geoffrey Haslam as producer. On the songs 'Superstar', 'Chapel Of Love', 'Daytime Hustler', 'Delta Dawn', 'Friends' and 'Leader Of The Pack' Barry played piano in a rhythm section of four. He provided solo piano accompaniment for the songs 'Do You Want To Dance' and 'Am I Blue'. He co-produced the second album which was simply titled *Bette Midler*.

Bette covered everything in her act. She sang torch songs, show tunes, pop standards with a difference, rock and blues and she delivered them with what had been described as a brassy, archly camp style. She was called 'the first cabaret star of the Beatle generation'.

Bette took a Grammy Award as Newcomer Of The Year in 1972. She was everything the critics and the fans wanted – no mean feat, to put it mildly!

The *New York Times* critic Chris Chase wrote on 14 January 1973:

Bette pushes her hair back, poses like early Rita Hayworth. She imitates Laura Nyro – speaking, not singing. She welcomes the front rows. Though she wouldn't do her act in front of her father ... there's nothing off-putting about it; her raffishness seems to come from a deep well of merriment, she has a gaiety and sweetness one seldom finds in a comic, man or woman.

And there's nothing she can't sing ... songs from the '40s, the '50s, the '60s.

And the American-published *Encyclopedia Of Pop, Rock and Soul* prefaces its entry for Bette with an uncredited quote:

She moves like her muscles are made of rubber. She moves like Charlie Chaplin. Her voice turns from silky soft to funky ...

For once the superlatives of show-biz magazines and journals, the record company press hand-out sheets and mouthings of critics quick to jump on the bandwagon had real substance. And indeed the lady's success has lasted into the eighties and she herself still possesses endless enthusiasm and energy packing one hell of a wallop in her shows. And Barry was there in the early days, something of an uncredited musical genius, for who and what else could stay the pace and serve the dynamism of this Jewish lady from Patterson?

Midler raved about his musical work for her. In a moment of humour she told famous club owner Lennie Sogoloff of the Turnpike Jazz Club on Route 1, Danvers: 'He even does jingles.' Barry was quick to counter with, 'The jingles bought my Steinway in my apartment.'

Sogoloff recognised the Manilow genius behind the Midler spectacular. Bette played his club following her engagement at Carnegie and Sogoloff gave himself a preview by attending the concert at the New York famous venue.

Sogoloff says: 'So, I'm sitting there on this night in June '72, when this piano player walked out wearing a costume that made him look like a doorman in a second-rate apartment house. Later, I found out he had rented the outfit.

'This kid played a couple of songs, one of which was "Mandy". He didn't sing then. I nudged my wife and said, "This must be the Barry Manilow we agreed to give 25 per cent of the billing in the contract." I was impressed. I took notes.' A wise man!

By this time Barry had begun evolving his own career. He performed a growing number of solo engagements as well as accompanying Bette and touring with her. Irv Biegel, then with Bell Records, later a vice-president of Millinium Records, signed Barry to a solo recording contract. Barry had his own named outfit called

34

Featherbed – or at least so he led everyone to believe! In fact Barry *was* Featherbed! He made a single for Biegel, with 'Could It Be Magic', one of his own compositions, as the B-side. The producer was Tony Orlando, an artist who enjoyed solo success with such songs as 'Bless You' and hits with Dawn 'Knock Three Times', 'Tie A Yellow Ribbon', 'Say, Has Anybody Seen My Sweet Gypsy Rose' and 'Who's In The Strawberry Patch With Sally' during the years 1971 to 1974. Orlando was a hot US pop name and it was thought he would help gain attention for Barry by producing him. Later the neglected B-side would give Barry a multi-million seller.

By 1973 Barry had his own very first album on the market and at the same time he began to play a more prominent part in the Midler show.

He opened the second half of her programme which he refers to as 'like following World War II' and the very first occasion on which he did this was in Columbia, Maryland. He was unbilled and unannounced. He did three songs. The audience loved them and they adored him. It was no mean feat and on the surface the very thought of following tempestuous dynamic Bette seemed crazy. It would have been for most artists. According to Sogoloff the inclusion of Barry arose from a discussion he had with Bette's manager, Norm Weiss, over a possible support or opening act.

'Let's not haggle about the opening act, Norm,' Sogoloff said. 'What about the kid piano player?'

Weiss merely muttered, 'Barry,' and Sogoloff replied, 'Why not? He could do two or three numbers with the drummer and bass player.'

And this he did.

Barry's audience response clearly laid the foundation for his future solo career and it certainly alerted record company personnel. His solo album did pretty well and went on selling over a considerable period of time. This is not surprising since wherever he went with Bette there followed sales in the local record stores.

By 1974 he was ready for a solo tour though there was initial uncertainty. He had mixed feelings and he told an American newspaper writer that though he was on his own he would rejoin Bette for another tour if she would phone and ask for him. Yet at the same time he said, 'Suppose I had a booking in Miami and she asked me to do a tour with her, I would have to refuse.' Bette at this time had more or less decided she would rest for a year and take stock of her situation before it got too much out of control. She was also worried by the danger for any artist who rises to the fore quickly with much trumpeting of skills and has to face the fact that she might burn herself out.

There were those who postulated that Barry and Bette had had a violent quarrel. It seemed the usual kind of rumour which invariably finds its way into print via the more 'muck spreading' type of journal. Barry comments: 'A lot of people think we had a fight, but we didn't. Our paths just split.'

Various testimonies have come from people associated with Barry and Bette during this period. One of Bette's original Harlette girls (Bette's accompanying girl backups) was Robin Grean and she has this to say about Barry:

Barry is an excellent musician, one of the finest I've ever worked with, and I've been working the New York Studios for a long time [Her father recorded with the Andrews Sisters]. He knows his music and teaches it well. It's odd, because when I first saw him at the Continental Baths, I thought he's a quiet sort of guy. Then he sang, and he's a good singer, but he has no great personality, he doesn't try to be a great personality on stage. He doesn't have this 'Here I am, I'm gonna be a star' attitude. But I was impressed with his music, his teaching us the parts. He had everything written out, but the other girls don't read music that much, so he ended up by teaching them by ear. The new things we did, like 'In The Mood' he had recorded with Bette, and he had written everything out for her. When Barry taught it to us, he had figured out which parts he was going to give each of us. He is a fascinating musician, because he knows exactly what he wants, and he knows how to teach it. Some people know, but have no way of conveying it to people who don't read music.

Another admirer of Barry's from this period is Sharon Redd, an American girl singer who hit the British disco charts in 1980, and who has sung with Patti La Belle, Lou Rawls, Bobby 'Blue' Bland, Petula Clark and Helen Reddy.

She told me of how she joined Bette's Harletts. 'I went for my audition and I said to Bette, "I have never heard of you." She was thrilled with the remark. "I like it honey," she said. I was in. And Barry Manilow was the MD.'

Sharon was full of praise for Barry both for his skill in training and arranging the girls and for his own musical mastery.

So Bette's year off gave Barry a time when he says he 'took up the ball and ran ... making albums, personal appearances, television guest spots' and one of the most important things he did was to find himself a top rate manager, and an equally proficient record company boss. The first was Miles Lourie. The second was Clive Davis. There was also the small matter of setting out on his first solo tour. The years 1974 and 1975 promised many things.

CLIVE, MILES AND '74 FIRST

It's 1981 and I'm on the line to Barry in California. I'm involved in writing a series on MOR Musical Greats for the *Manchester Evening News*, Britain's biggest provincial evening newspaper. So I mention some important details from Barry's past and wonder whether some of the accompanying publicity to those events owes more to a lively publicist than reality.

One story concerns Clive Davis and a meeting he had with Barry after the star's first tour had been completed. It centres around a song called 'Brandy' which had been penned by Scott English and Richard Kerr. Barry and the others decide it should be called 'Mandy' and he goes into the studio to record the song. Clive Davis comes as well and he sits next to the piano. The recording session finishes and Clive says some much quoted words: 'Oh, it's wonderful, wonderful! Barry, if you have a hit with this ballad your career is made!'

So, did it happen? And that way? 'Sure, it was a great moment. He was right in what he said!' He was. The single 'Mandy' hit the charts and then, 'it went faster than anything, it just jumped and kept on jumping up the charts.' It was an American number one in just over a month. The airwaves were saturated with 'Mandy'. In just eight months from turning solo Barry was riding high.

Davis was the head of records at Arista, formerly Bell Records, and oddly enough he was, like Barry, from Brooklyn. His was a legendary name in record industry circles in America and in the rest of the world. He had become boss of the massive CBS company in 1965 and under his care were such high-selling recording acts as Dylan, Simon & Garfunkel, Blood Sweat & Tears, Janis Joplin and at times, it seemed just about everybody who was anything in the record world was signed up with CBS.

In the mid-1970s he left CBS and then founded Arista. He rid himself of all his former artists except for Britain's teenybop heroes from Scotland, the Bay City Rollers; Melissa Manchester; and most wisely Barry M. Later Arista would boast Patti Smith, Alan Parsons, Iggy Pop, Eric Carmen, Gil Scott-Heron and the Kinks, to name just a handful. For the most part the artist roster and the general product reflected quality and taste with only the Rollers as a major exception: they were part of the instant money making teen scene and were seen as successors to The Monkees and The Beatles.

Obviously though when Davis was setting out with the new company, Arista, in 1974 it was a case of quickly assessing the artist situation and then deciding on immediate action. The name of Barry Manilow was paramount. It was a right choice for with Barry: Arista went places. Davis of course knew the market and those whose job it is to promote and programme music were people who knew that if Davis was behind someone then more than likely there was a superstar in the making. And Manilow made their ears prick up. One person who was not surprised at the reception for Barry was Miles Lourie. Lourie had become Barry's lawyer-manager, the duality of role being very much accepted in the 1970s record business world. Originally Lourie had been a very able trial lawyer but in the early 1960s he became interested in the music business. He founded his own firm in 1966 and among clients before Barry there were household names like Simon & Garfunkel, James Taylor and Ray Charles. Lourie became Barry's manager after a spell as his attorney.

Lourie, though, sees his roles as clear and defined. 'When Barry started talking to me about possible management I had to decide how I should become a manager. I chose to become one overtly not covertly. I have different letterheads for the two businesses. I keep them totally separate. I never give free legal advice as a manager. I don't manage somebody that I represent as a lawyer and I don't act as a lawyer for somebody that I represent as a manager.'

The US trade paper *Record World* asked Miles in 1977 whether he found it difficult to change the image of Barry and so take him out of his known and established role as arranger and conductor. He replied:

Well, it was a two-fold attack as with any new act. It's not a secret – one is by records and one is by personal appearances. Barry had already had experience in the studio – he had co-produced one or two of Bette's records. He spent a lot of time in studios both in connection with commercials and with phonograph records. So it was a question of having the records come out under his own name. Then he appeared on tour … I don't think his success was hindered too much by the fact that he had been an arranger, producer, musical director before that. In fact, he had some degree of acceptance due to his involvement with Bette on stage and on records. I don't think it was our major problem.

So what were those problems? Lourie names adjustment for one. He drew a picture of Barry on stage with Bette under the classiest of conditions and linking the two halves of the show. And then suddenly, he says, there was Barry having the first half of a show to himself in less exotic surroundings and without the mass of faces out there in front, not that it was long before Barry played only prestigious venues.

Lourie told *Record World* how one of the arts of management is the balancing act between an artist's inaccessibility and his public accessibility. 'It's also a question of gearing that balance to the market place that the artist's appealing to. The balance would be different with a rock and roll act than it would be with a top forty contemporary performer, because their venues tend to be very different.' Lourie said Barry would never play Madison Square Garden, the famous massive concert and entertainment venue in New York, simply because his art is not directed toward that vast kind of auditorium. Lourie also commented that a manager and artist must be careful in deciding which kinds of media should be exploited in addition to making records and live appearances. He felt at this time, in 1977, Barry should think seriously about film, theatre and television, although of course Barry had had some experience of this world when he wrote the music for *The Drunkard*.

Irv Biegel is quoted as saying that Barry made 'one of the best moves he's ever made in his career' by utilising the services of Miles Lourie. 'And I think ... the success ... a lot has to be attributed to Miles Lourie. The way Barry's career was handled: with kid gloves!'

Both Clive Davis and Miles Lourie had much they could be pleased with from Barry's first-ever solo tour in 1974. It was the beginning of the solo Barry which would eventually lead Lourie to comment: 'Barry could put out an album of forty minutes of silence and it would sell a million copies.' And he would later comment: 'The well-spring of his career is performing – marketing the product – and we've got to continually feed the waters of interest ... The name of the game is emotion, in a sense, he fulfils a need. His music helps people through very difficult times in their lives.'

For his first tour Barry decided he would engage Bette's star-studded, talent-ridden Harlettes. It began in Boston. The audience was under fifty. The following night it was four times the size. And Barry never looked back. The word quickly spread that this guy really had an act, that he wasn't just a fill-in capable of a pifling three numbers, that he was a man whose voice could charm all through a ninety-minute show, and that he was highly skilled on the keyboards.

The tour achieved exactly what his record company desired – extra record sales and a general media buzz. Barry was well on his way – to the top. The hits were to follow, fast and furious ...

'75, HITSVILLE AND ONWARDS

'Mandy' topped the US charts in 1975. It made No. 11 in the British listings on 15 March. Britain then proceeded with surprising caution. Barry had no more chart singles in the UK until 1978. But, boy oh boy, America acted quite differently.

While 'Mandy' topped the US singles' chart another single, 'It's A Miracle', was released. It shot without hesitation to the top spot. In June it was followed by 'Could It Be Magic' and Barry, ever-conscious of standards, had also by then rushed his back-up ladies, now known as The Flashy Ladies, together with his band City Rhythm into the studios and had remixed four of the cuts from his debut album *Barry Manilow*. 'One Of These Days', 'Oh My Lady', 'Sweet Life' and 'Could It Be Magic' received the new treatment.

During the summer of 1975 he laid down a new album which was eventually titled *Tryin' To Get The Feeling*. This was released in October and within a month it was riding high. And another number one chart single was on its way with Barry's recording of sometime Beach Boy Bruce Johnstone's 'I Write The Songs'. Incredible though it may appear, over in the UK it was former teen throb David Cassidy who scored with the song in the top twenty. You could hear the Manilow fan hisses for miles.

Further US hits were 'This One's For You', 'Weekend In New England', 'Looks Like We Made It', 'Daybreak', 'Can't Smile Without You', 'Even Now', 'Copacabana', 'Somewhere In The Night', 'Ready To Take A Chance Again', 'Ships', 'When I Wanted You', 'I Don't Want To Walk Without You' and 'I Made It Through The Rain'. The latter charted in the winter of 1980 to end a remarkable six-year hit cycle.

And from the spring of 1977 until the winter of 1980 Barry's success included eight albums each of which sold over a million copies as *Barry Manilow I*, *Barry Manilow II* (already previous sellers but picked up major sales once Barry's career advanced), *One Voice*, *Tryin' To Get The Feeling*, *This One's For You*, *Even Now*, *Barry Manilow – Greatest Hits* and *Barry Manilow Live*. Of these there were three million sales for *Tryin' To Get The Feeling*, *This One's For You*, *Even Now* and *Barry Manilow – Greatest Hits* and the *Live* album sold a totally mind-boggling four million copies in America alone.

In 1977 there were five albums on the charts simultaneously – a record only achieved by just two other singers, Frank Sinatra and Johnny Mathis. At the last estimated count in late 1980 record sales were claimed as in excess of 27 million. In the UK, 1978 was the only year which to any extent gave the American superstar fair recognition. 'Can't Smile Without You', 'Somewhere In The Night' linked with 'Copacabana' charted but only in the lower forties while 'Could It Be Magic' did reach 25 but went no further. 1980 was kinder with 'Lonely Together' reached 22 and a year later 'Bermuda Triangle' reached 15. None-the-less all this makes pretty poor reading when placed next to Barry's success in the United States. Doubtless one reason for the disparity lies in the artist's rare visits to the UK and the British radio set-up which makes it hard for the Manilow type of artist to gain major airplay. At least though Manilow's albums have fared much better.

But America saw lots of Barry, whether in live concert, or on the TV screen, while endless US radio stations pumped out his music day and night. His face adorned the magazines. He was a favourite pin-up.

Barry himself was frequently stunned by the demand for his records. After 'Mandy' took a mere six weeks to hit No. 1 he said, 'When I found out "Mandy" was at No. 1 I was scared stiff. How was I supposed to follow that? What I finally realised was that what people wanted was not just a nice record. They were getting out of this song a personality. There was a person singing this song. He was moving them.'

Others said his records were bridging the age gap and they thought he did this more successfully than several other names. Two fellow contenders which were brought forward were Elton John and Tony Orlando. Elton, though, was rather bizarre in his dress and older people found this rather disquieting, even to their sensibilities distasteful. Tony Orlando had flourished as a solo singer and with his group Dawn but the latter displayed little of the earthiness which was associated with Orlando's early days. Barry was termed the last of the Great White Hopes. There was considerable discussion in teen journals as to whether the teens bought his music. Many of them did.

Not surprisingly there were some critics and they still exist. One of the unexpected critics of Manilow was the famous US singer Tony Bennett. He was reported as saying, in *Radio Times*:

Barry Manilow? Guys like him come out of the ice-box. I mean there's a whole group of guys like that. Tons of them. They're always around, and they change with the seasons.

47

More charitable fans busied themselves searching the charts for these ice-box spawnings. They reported no sign of others and so questioned the basic statement. Other fans waxed indignant. One of the insulted fans in Britain was Anne McDonald who penned her views for the magazine *Prelude*:

Everyone is entitled to an opinion. But honestly, where has this person *been* for the past five years?

When checking his own album positions in the American charts has he *never* noticed Barry's name up there along with all the 'greats'? (In 1977 Barry had five albums in the charts at the same time!)

Has he never heard of Barry's string of American awards won steadily (and amazingly) over the last three years? (e.g. Entertainer of the Year, Top Pop Vocalist, etc.) And has he *never* heard (or what is more important listened to) 'Even Now' or 'Copacabana' or – or – (I could go on forever!)

That his own personal taste does not include B.M. is obvious (hard to believe – but true) but how anyone, especially a fellow American, can be totally unaware of such success is beyond me.

I don't suppose Mr Bennett had these words thrust before him but the *Prelude* caption writer said it all: 'This One's For You, Tony Bennett' and it might be said to all others who put B.M. down with such starkness, even foolishness.

Barry puts the whole record success story down to an accident. 'I was going to be an arranger. That's what I was doing for Bette and that's what I thought I'd be doing for the rest of my life. Singing was a total surprise to me.

'It all happened after I had written some songs, nothing special. Then one day Ron Dante heard one of my tunes. "Why don't we record it?" I really didn't want to do it, to start a whole new career. I was twenty-seven at the time. But I did it.

'I was surprised when I heard my voice on record. I never thought it would sell. If Ron had sung on the demo then I might never have started.'

And B.M. would have remained busying himself composing and arranging, lending some vocal aid on self-composed commercials. He would have been rich but not nearly as rich as he has become through the success of his hit singles and albums.

'It was pure luck and determination which got me started, and the chance meeting with Bette Midler.' And there was the time already mentioned when he finally sang to her audience rather than charmed them on the piano. 'I was sure the minute I walked out on stage the audience were going to throw tomatoes ... Nobody was more surprised than me when nobody threw a thing at me!' Girls rushed the stage.

'My music is well thought out – adult, professional tunes. All I'm really trying to do is bring back intelligent music. I haven't figured out my *style* yet. But I'm on to something that a lot of people are getting off on!' This is what he said toward the end of the seventies.

In the interview which he gave me for the *Manchester Evening News* early summer of 1981 he said this of his singing and of his attitude towards his music.

Yes, people have said I was a new Bacharach. It's flattering and I think some have added a touch of Leon Russell and Bo Diddley. Well, that's what I wanted but hopefully all in the background, their styles influencing but not dominating.

And true to form Barry expressed his own feeling of inadequacy at times: 'If you have a hit, then your career can be all right. Clive Davis was right about me,

y. I mean my records charted at a time when
ere not too popular. The Top Twenty was very
rock orientated and now once more in the eighties the
American scene has become that way again.

'Once it was so-called acid rock and now it's hard rock
or whatever. It's not easy to push my kind of music into
that kind of world.' And of course he could have added an
extra difficulty which is this – when a certain kind of
music dominates the charts then DJs and programmers
(who decide which music will be played on a show) tend to
go with the popular music. It means others get less
needle-time. Somehow, doubtless talent is the reason,
Barry Manilow has survived in spite of this.

'At first I did very little. My success seems as though it
came very quickly. It did once the first hit came but it
wasn't automatic in the beginning. Whatever, I just go on
writing and writing, wherever I am. I think whatever the
song, whatever the record, the important thing is that I
stay true to myself.

'I think being truthful is important. What I do, where I
go, I live my life that way. It affects my music. Sometimes
when the pressure is on I start to think, am I terrible? Am
I less talented? I do not like being categorised in my
music, my records. I am one person, that's all!'

He would probably appreciate the analysis of him made
by British writer Bill Field of the Barnet Press Group who
wrote;

Manilow's appeal cuts right across the age-barriers.
Whether he is singing his own songs or other people's,
his performances always have the polish of sheer
professionalism not only in the singing but also in the
arrangements and the whole presentation of the music.

Ballads are undoubtedly one of Manilow's strongest
points ... But Barry is a long way from being just a
ballad singer – he is an all-round entertainer.

And Barry Manilow has retained his freshness by always broadening his repertoire of originals to include material penned by others. He constantly looks for new sources in song and new styles for recording. As for the question of whether he should record some pop classics he is uncertain: 'It's always in the back of my mind, but I'm still not sure what the point would be; I don't know if my audience would connect.' At the same time he is ever-ready to hear new material, and he is particularly interested in British writers.

He says: 'It's exactly what I wanted. All my albums are filled with everything I learned – a piece of show-business, a piece of theatre, a piece of rock and roll, a piece of jazz. The first time I released an album, they said you can't do that, you gotta make a record that sounds the same throughout, that can be put in a category so everybody can sell you right. But my background is so diversified. I figured I'd do what was right for me. I don't think there's anyone else doing quite what I'm doing.

'It's a personal thing. My records are more personal than the other guy's. I coproduce them myself, and no matter how commercial they sound, I try to get a *person* across. There are a couple of spots on all the albums where my voice cracks or I don't sing exactly right or I sigh a little bit or I pop on the microphone, and I choose to leave them in. If I were listening out there myself, I would be interested in hearing a human being.'

'If you judge my work only by my singles,' he told *Circus* magazine, in 1978, 'then I guess I've had some awfully sweet, romantic singles, but I don't think there's anything wrong with romantic music. It's doing something for somebody. I used to love to make out to Johnny Mathis' music. If somebody is making out to my music, I think that's terrific.

'I don't think I'm saccharine. I put myself and other people down when they get too saccharine. I take it to the limit. I'll admit that. Even I, in the recording studio, fall to my knees on the key change, and I write the songs. And it still sounds like the Bible, or something, but it's effective.'

Not surprisingly, when considering the money they stand to earn and have earned, various writers who have penned material for his records have little but praise for Barry. Yet in spite of this obvious financial inducement, two of Barry's writers speak with ringing sincerity of their admiration for him as an artist.

Gerard Kenny says: 'I play my piano and I write my songs. I walked into the office and I met Barry. He was so nice to me. I just thought I'm the lucky one to have my song recorded. I don't suppose I thought he might record a song of mine. So the big thrill in my life was going into my music publisher, Chappells in London, and hearing he's taken a song of mine. He's recorded "Made It Through The Rain" and "Nickles and Dimes". And he's recording my song called "Fantasy".'

Geoff Murrow is another who speaks highly of Barry and quite apart from financial gratification seems genuinely honoured that the American star should record his music. His big song for Barry was 'Can't Smile Without You'.

I met him early in the summer of 1981 in the office of a new British record company with whom he has close associations – Recorded Delivery. Also present was Geoff's son, as if to keep an eye on his dad's activities or, at any rate, revel in his father's undoubted enthusiasm for music. During our talk Geoff played a new song which he has written with Barry in mind. The tape had by this date winged its way across the Atlantic and Geoff had his fingers crossed. Certainly it was tailor-made for Barry's vocal inflections and mannerisms.

Geoff was at one time teamed up with David Martin and Chris Arnold. Martin had achieved success as a songwriter and producer with a lot of hits to his credit. He himself had started as a solo singer when he was only sixteen years old. By the time he reached the advanced age of eighteen though, he was more more-or-less resigned to the fact that he wasn't going to make it as a junior chart-topper. So he concentrated on writing and with Geoff and Chris they had songs recorded by such artists as Frank Ifield, Dusty Springfield, Cliff Richard, Cilla Black, Edison Lighthouse and even the 'King' of rock 'n' roll himself – Elvis. The trio had the distinction of being the first British songwriters to write for Elvis. The song was 'Just A Little Bit Of Green'.

In 1976 the team produced 'Can't Smile Without You' which David recorded for British DJM, the company which published the Beatles' songs and released all the early Elton John records. It meant precisely nothing – as far as radio programmers were concerned and of course, the great British public.

The record was issued in the States and it was heard on US radio. A number of artists picked up the song and made their own recording. One major star who added the song to his vast repertoire was Perry Como.

Geoff says: 'The big big break came when an artist called Gino Cunico recorded the song. He was with Arista, the company whose MD was Clive Davis and who had Barry on their artist roster. Clive heard the record and he thought a great deal of it. He ordered it should be sent to Barry.

'As far as I know the first reaction of Barry was straightforward. He said, "I hate it," which was a little upsetting, I suppose for us! Anyway, Clive insisted Barry gave it another go. He told Barry it was a "hit" song. It was what we thought, after all!

'Clive said to Barry, "Do it," and it was recorded and it was released. The rest is history. I met Barry some time afterwards. He said, "Thank you for the song," and he meant it. He's a lovely, lovely fellow.

'His voice is quite extraordinary. He can take an ordinary song and make it mean something. He very often records songs by people who until that moment are not rated.

'I heard the news that Barry had recorded the song when I visited Arista UK. I was absolutely bowled over. You always yearn for a major artist to take a song and here it was happening for us.

"And then within such a short time, a few weeks, there was even more mind-boggling news, the record had charted. It was an exciting day when Barry's recording was flown over and we heard it.'

Geoff, like many people in the British music world, is puzzled as to why Barry has not enjoyed greater success than he has in Britain. He believes it may well be due to the lack of real exposure of middle-of-the-road music on UK radio. He feels America is much more orientated toward Barry's music but none-the-less he feels that Barry can only sell more and more records as time goes by. Certainly Barry himself, from my conversation with him, knows he has many followers in Britain but he is also aware that he must spend more time here – but then his time is limited and so many countries desire his presence. It's very much a complicated game for the American superstar.

In 1975 Barry sold over four million singles and 1.6 million in the US. The awards flowed in. He was Top New Male Vocalist for Singles and Albums according to US trade papers *Cashbox* and *Record World*. *Radio & Records* said he was their Pop Artist Of The Year award winner while he was the Top New Male Artist for *Music Retailer*. The following year saw continued success with Geoff Murrow's effort high in the ranking list. His fourth album *This One's For You* had a cool half-a-million orders even before it hit the shops and the year later, in 1977, came the moment when five of his albums were chart-listed at one and the same time. The fifth was the double-record live set which contained stage takes of all his hit singles and, making its debut on vinyl, Barry's assortment of early commercial numbers under the 'Very Strange Medley' title.

The LP was recorded live at the Uris Theatre in New York City in December, 1976, mid-way through the mammoth ninety eight-city tour of the US which ran from July 1976 until April 1977. Barry tried to represent on disc some of the excitement which accompanied the concerts.

At the end of 1977 Barry won the American Music Award as Favourite Pop-Rock Vocalist, his single 'I Can't Smile Without You' was in the Top Ten of the pop charts, No. 1 on the east listening chart and became his fourth gold single. He ended the year with 'Daybreak' riding high, the album *Even Now* went gold within four weeks and there was a Top Ten smash with the title cut, 'Copacabana' which gave him enormous popularity in the discos. The Film, *Foul Play* boosted sales of 'Ready To Take A Chance'. Manilow's albums sold three million copies within the space of the first ten weeks of 1978. It was enough to make anyone wonder, in view of all this success, the TV engagements (particularly *The Second Barry Manilow Special* on ABC-TV, which happened at the end of February 1978) and general promotional activities, how he found time to compose.

Even Now had Barry whistling an introduction to 'Can't Smile Without You', saw him hitting the top of his vocal range for the beginning of 'I Just Want To Be The One In Your Life', had his up-tempo number 'Copacabana' with its Latin funk rhythm, ballads 'Leavin' In The Morning', 'A Linda Song' and 'Starting Again'. Running the full gamut of emotions the album contained an angry 'I Was A Fool (To Let You Go)', the bitter-sweetness of the 'Starting Again' and what writer Peter Reilly called the 'softly dappled reverie' of 'Sunrise'.

Reilly commented for *Stereo Review*, June, 1978:

> In everything Manilow performs he has a tough, city grace about him – like Cagney hoofing it in the old flicks, or George Burns doing a monologue about yesterdays on the Lower East Side. Like them, he's also very proud of his profession, and how well he's done it. He has every reason to be.

Los Angeles writer Dave Blume said *Even Now* confirmed even more Manilow's knack of violating time-honoured notions of hit making:

> According to industry guidelines, a hit record should have immediate impact. It may shout, scold or whisper, but it must be instantly compelling. Manilow doesn't seem to reach for those emotional outer limits that imply truth and conviction. He just sings the songs.

Manilow, he said, had boy-next-door ingenuousness which made him stand out among the multitude of singers who were vying for radio programming.

In America *Even Now* sold a cool three million. The sales were still there for the 1979 release *One Voice* where there was an even greater emphasis on ballads. However there was a *rock* ballad, 'Ships', a number given popularity by Ian Hunter, one-time lead singer of Mott The Hoople and also a solo artist, US trade giant *Billboard* commented:

> Overall the quality is high, thanks in part to the tasteful orchestrations by Artie Butler and Manilow's rhythm track arrangements ...

'Ships' was one of three songs which came from outside sources. The other two were Gino Cunico's 'When I Wanted You' and a number popularised in the 1940s by Helen Forest and Harry James entitled 'I Don't Want To Walk Without You'.

The *Billboard* reviewer did not appreciate 'two glitzy disco-tinged numbers on side two which shamelessly copy "Copacabana"'.

For Barry fans the album *One Voice* was another spellbinding affair. No one could have been more enthusiastic than British fan Gillian who wrote in the journal *Prelude*:

I've got it you know! *One Voice*. I can only describe it as a wonderful experience. I called at the shop where I had a copy ordered on the 29th September, but they didn't have it! My chin hit the floor. October 3rd. I rang again, and yes, they had it, (WOW!!) but with it being Wednesday, they'd be closed half-day from 1 pm and it was already 12.30, and to get to my favourite record shop takes 1½ hours and two bus journeys, so my chin hit the floor again! The bloke on the other end of the phone must have heard the thud, and he probably detected a slight cry in my voice too, cos he said, 'Well, if it's so important to you, although the shop will be closed, I'll be working, so if would like to come down town, I'll let you in.' I couldn't believe it. By this time, I already had one foot outside the door with a fiver in my hand. So I dashed all the way there on the two buses and got soaked! (It was raining you see.) But my tough journey was well rewarded because 1½ hours later I held it in my trembling hands – my very own copy of *One Voice* (Sigh!). It was all very dramatic – even the bloke in the shop had a tear in his eye (or was it water from the broken gutter he was standing under?) as I thanked him for his kind act and understanding. So, clutching it tightly to my bosom, I dashed all the way back to Anfield. Two buses and a lot more rain I reached home and placed it on the turntable. Lay back in my favourite chair, and just let it all wash over me. My earlobes just wobbled with pleasure.

But if it should be supposed that Manilow fans merely take whatever the star offers then the same *Prelude* issue which contained Gillian's adventure also printed this comment from Lorraine Corless of Lancaster:

The offending track is 'Why Don't We Try A Slow Dance'. It starts off with a fantastic disco beat and then changes to a very slow fifties-ish ballad. It is very cleverly done but I find it too sugary sweet. Barry comes over best in the 1940 boogie songs or his own brand of ballads where he can give the song his full treatment.

Overall, though, Lorraine really liked the album with its seven compositions penned by the artist himself and certainly, like her, many critics raved over the cut 'Who's Been Sleeping In My Bed' with its up-tempo feel, interesting lyrics and general catchy air. There was also much praise for the song entitled 'Bobbie Lee' about a young girl who leaves home for city bright lights.

In 1979 Arista released *Manilow Magic: The Best of Barry Manilow*. It certainly widened the artist's potential audience and built upon the great reaction the artist had received when he visited the UK during the autumn of 1978.

Much more meaningful for Barry's fans was his new 1980 album entitled *Barry*. Seven of the ten tracks were co-written and it was all put together during spring 1980. Four tracks were used in the world tour. The album contained 'Lonely Together', the track which became his long-awaited major British hit (it reached 22) and which took a mere two hours to record. It was written by Kenny Nolan. As Barry says, 'It's usually the simpler songs that get to be the hits.' Production was by Barry since his long-standing and regular co-producer, Ron Dante, was busy in New York co-producing *Children Of A Lesser God*, a Broadway theatre hit.

I Made It Through The Rain was another album cut with a

similiar style to 'Mandy' or 'Somewhere In The Night'. This was the first track from the album to be culled for US single release. A drum beat from Ed Green gave 'Dance Away' its introduction while 'Bermuda Triangle' (a UK single hit in 1981) was almost Hawaiian in its basic rhythmic beat. Writers Richard Kerr and John Bettis of 'One Voice' and 'Where Are They Now' fame penned side two's opening track, 'Life Will Go On'. There's a fine piece of Barry's piano-playing on 'Only In Chicago'. He performed a tongue-in-cheek version of 'The Last Duet' with his guest Lily Tomlin and the song was in fact a mild skit on the duo pop successes of that time, John Travolta and Olivia Newton-John and Neil Diamond and Barbra Streisand.

The last track was particularly interesting since it was another film track with which Barry was associated. Co-written with Sussman and Feldman it was 'We Still Have Time', from the Jack Lemmon/Robby Benson film *Tribute*. Connoisseurs noted there were no tracks, unlike past days, which featured writing from Enoch and Adrienne Anderson while the Manilow/Panzer writing partnership, previously so fertile, had only come up with one cut. Forty-two musicians received album credit with Barry and backing vocalists included. Naturally worldwide the album has sold a few million.

And then came renewed Arista/Ariola TV advertising for the album in early summer 1981 – it had already been on the UK charts for six months but obviously the company felt there were countless thousands still there waiting to be reached. A £300,000 campaign was launched between 25 May and 14 June with a blitz of ads including footage from his BBC TV specials. Arista estimated the ad campaign would mean 80 per cent of all adult viewers in the testing Anglia area would see the commercial at least five times. Record shops were supplied with full point of sale and merchandising back-up including centrepieces, posters, window-banners and special display packs.

And of course the story goes on. As a whole Barry's recording career has been a spectacular success. Barry says disarmingly: 'I never expected to be paid as a singer … I'm a pop singer who dabbles in the rock 'n' roll field. There's a certain inherent rhythm I can't deny I adore. But I'm not a rock singer. A rock singer is Mick Jagger. I'd much rather be what I am … I'm serious about what I'm doing … This is *it* for me. I'm trying to contribute something.'

.Certainly he is his music. When he sings he is transformed. He takes off. He captures this on his records. It's a view well espoused by Chip Orton in the US magazine *Us*. Under the journal's general heading of Romantic Music, Orton writes:

No singer since Sinatra has done as much for the romantic ballad. And Manilow hasn't had it easy, cutting a swath through the chart-dominating sounds of rock and disco. Today Manilow is providing a good deal more than back-seat mood music. Other romantic singers have managed a few hits, but no one can match Manilow's output … it's an unparalleled track record.

Orton also commented:

John Denver, Andy Gibb and Olivia Newton-John can be as heartwarming, as sly, as ingratiating; Billy Joel and Neil Diamond can push a tougher street-smart sensuality; Barbra Streisand can surpass his ability to uncover nuances of feeling. But the synthesis of all these elements into a unique style is Manilow's alone.

Barry Manilow has of course had his critics, indeed some would say most of the musical press has had a go at him at some time or other. Orton refers to American carpers who condemn him for opening the floodgates of musical marshmallow: 'They jeer at his looks and label him Barry Vanilla, king of middle of the road.'

Britain's arch-carver of Manilow is seen by some people as former *Daily Mail* music writer Simon Kinnersley. In November 1980 he wrote words in this top-selling British paper which had Manilow fans in danger of suffering fatal heart attacks:

> But where does his success stem from? Is he a performer of genuine originality and ability, or a boy from the back streets of New York who just got lucky? His success has come at a time when the pop industry has been in turmoil. As punk, new wave and disco have come and gone, he has continued to offer a consistently safe and unchanging style of music.
>
> With bland orchestral arrangements wrapped solidly around his songs, he has continued to cater for the frequently ignored middle of the road pop market ...
>
> If Olivia Newton-John has cornered the nice-girl-next-door market then the male counterpoint has been swept up with great opportunism by the sincere Mr Manilow. He has become the Doris Day of the 80s.
>
> Presenting a solid asexual image, Manilow neither threatens nor excites ...

Also less than appreciative was Simon Frith in *Melody Maker*, who on 17 February 1979, when reviewing *Manilow Magic: The Best Of Barry Manilow*, commented:

> Technically he's a dull singer, with little variation of tempo and mood, with none of the subtlety that characterizes the great pop balladeers. Manilow is in the bland Andy Williams tradition, though he's less pretty. He sings through his nose, slightly garbled, slightly flat, and conveys particular intimacy. His very lack of technique makes him sound sincere. His records have a smothering emotional flow.

Manilow himself is a dim figure – his records certainly don't explore his own emotions. But he's also a figure dim enough to represent romantic idiology. His ballads all sound like film tracks because he works with Hollywood's gently swirling themes of love and hope.

But as Manilow has said, 'Critics, bah! What do they want me to do? … I like the romantic records I make and the people I make them for. I stand behind my stuff as strongly as Led Zeppelin stands behind its music. I never thought I would be put down as being the most commercial piece of crap ever to hit the airwaves …'

Still, Barry's success shows that millions believe he is the greatest, whatever some may say.

MANILOW ON STAGE

He was there on stage and he was wearing the expected white sports coat, black silk trousers and a black silk open-collared shirt.

The fans went berserk. The rain poured down but it didn't dampen the way they felt. The event was in the open air so everyone was soaked and got progressively wetter. No one noticed, perhaps they would later as they squelched their way from a stadium filled with saturated grass and felt the coldness of their clothes against their skin. For now and for the ensuing two hours of concert it was Barry and just Barry. They would travel with him through what he termed the 'pain, agony, emotion part'. They would love his accordion spot and they would laugh as he played current rock hits of the moment like Rod Stewart's 'Do Ya Think I'm Sexy?' They would swoon as he re-entered for the second part of the show wearing an all-white suit and riding an exotically coloured float. He would sing the old-time commercials which first alerted people to his writing and vocal talents and he would tell and sing of another activity of his, producing a new album for Dionne Warwick.

'Sometimes in my show, I talk too much, I blab. I try stoppin' myself but when I'm out there it's like I'm sittin' in my living room talkin' to friends,' he told reporter

Tony Kornheiser of the *Philadelphia Enquirer*. He knows that the critics who delighted in carving him up were particularly prone to criticise this 'blab' but then the fans loved it. And anyway they see so little of him and they can't be with him where they wanted, in his actual real living room. And they knew right from the beginning that he was shy, reticent and reserved and he would be adverse to live shows and touring.

Even seasoned music-biz pros were slightly stunned when Barry announced a ninety-eight city tour of the United States. The tour dragged on for nine months. Lee Gurst said it was 'blood, sweat, and tears; craziness and insanity and nerves – a lot of things!'

The tour ran from July 1976 to April 1977. Barry's only previous tour had lasted six months – it was his 'breaking in' and had begun with a mere forty people at Boston's Paul's Mall and had ended with Barry and the Harlettes playing before large and appreciative audiences. Things had got better week by week.

The second tour put Barry firmly and squarely on the American music map. A mammoth tour like this, with a nightly stage performance may not have been Barry's idea of heaven in view of his generally retiring nature but it certainly made thousands of American fans deliriously happy. Even some of the newspaper and magazine critics admitted that Barry Manilow was more than a recording studio creation.

His stage act was slickly paced. There were costumes, slides, strobes, choreography, coloured lights and exploding smoke pots. On stage with him was Lady Flash, his own vocal group. They provided back-ups, gyrations, legs, titillation, definite touches of the saucy, and an initial show introduction. Lady Flash sang a Latin version of 'Some Day My Prince Will Come' and included within their performance bits and pieces of Barry's hit songs before the dramatic arrival of the star himself.

Barry frequently expressed his amazement at the reception he received during the long trek. He kept recalling the past and then simply being startled by the present. 'It's only been three years. If you got up on stage and three years later 11,000 people were screaming your name you'd be surprised too.' Barry also observed: 'When I play an arena you'll see them jumping on the car. It's very frightening from where I'm sitting. They're tryin' to turn the car over and you just want them to get out of the way. I don't know why they do that. They're just caught up in their own excitement, I guess. I don't do anything to merit that.'

The show was almost two-and-a-half hours in length with one interval. The repertoire varied from 1940s songs to contemporary music. Barry ad-libbed quite often and talked of places he had visited on the tour and if the chatter was often to the stage floor it was a habit which endeared him more and more to his fans. He sang his hits. Numerous reviewers commented on how he seemed to live out what must have been a childhood fantasy. They remarked on his boyish innocence and 'the attitude of how-did-all-this-ever-happen-to me' and they picked up on a remark like 'We're doing everything we know, so call the baby-sitters.' Observers said his ballads went down best and that once he launched into 'Weekend in New England' or 'I Write The Songs' the audiences fell apart in appreciation.

Mitchell Fink, a writer in Los Angeles, thought the Manilow show clearly displayed that he was 'the master of modulation, expertly crafted key changes that do much more than just hook the listener's attention. They've made his career what it is.' Fink concluded his review in the *Los Angeles Examiner* by saying, 'I've seen Manilow perform countless times over the last few years, and although I've never been a dyed-in-the-wool fan, I've never seen him give a bad performance. In the end Barry

Manilow is a talent I must respect.'

Chicago News journalist Richard Christiansen simply began his review by asking:

> Is it any wonder that all four of Barry Manilow's concerts through Saturday night are sold out? The man is something of an entertainment miracle himself, a combination of true grit, rhinestone glitz and basic schmaltz so smartly packaged and splashily produced that he all but overpowers his audience in a contemporary vaudeville extravaganza.

And Barry? To critics he said: 'They all criticised my show at the Uris Theatre in December. But not one of them said that there were 4,000 screaming fans falling out of their seats. My two week stand in New York was sold out two weeks in advance. Critics! I used to respect them until I realised the people I was being insulted by were people who knew much less than I do. I can't take them seriously.' And when asked why he was engaged in a nine-month, stamina-sapping extravaganza he replied: 'Today you've got to do more than compose and record. You have to get out there and sell if you want the big brass ring. Don't ask me why I'm doing it. Actually I know why. You've got to do it once. I decided I would undertake this tour to show my face to all those people who have bought so many of my records. I should say thank you to the country once. The only way is actually going on the road.'

Fortunately for his fans in the States and certainly for his British admirers, who at that time were starving for an appearance, he did set out once again on tour, this time one of six months. It included Britain and in the old country there was great expectancy and then eventual pandemonium when he hit the British shores.

Not long before Barry arrived in Britain he played at the Riviera, Las Vegas. This concert, in the so-called show-biz capital of the States, was something of a landmark in his career.

At the Riviera Barry was supported by Lady Flash and a new American comedian of the time, David Sayh. He exhibited what *Variety* magazine called the 'somebody' self-confidence:

> The production has gained considerably from new novelties; the obvious camp inserts throughout 'Jump Shout Boogie' medley, the piano bar 'Dew Drop Inn' sequence and, glitteringly, in illustrating his disc hit 'Copacabana'.
>
> The refreshingly frank sex thrusts, kidding or otherwise of Lady Flash are used best in 'Copacabana' where they parody a line number as chorus dolls with Manilow deliberately taking up the deliberately dumb terps and theme exceedingly well. The ladies and the star hit it off with elan throughout making the current Manilow edition fun to watch ...

The British journal *Record Business* was at the London Palladium event two months later. Editor Brian Mulligan thought that with Humperdinck in recording decline, Neil Diamond virtually retired and Jack Jones 'too classy by half', the time was ripe for Barry. He was impressed, all the more so because Barry's live reputation was unproven in the UK. He saw the Manilow show as a 'genuine visual experience, Las Vegas style' and the artist's work deserving of the standing ovation.

Manilow himself expressed surprise that his six London Palladium concerts sold out within days. 'It astonishes me. I do not know how or why it's happened, because I have never performed here before.'

British fans had a long wait for his next visit though the more keen had busily taken in American concerts. One of these was Jane Marsh. She was in no doubt:

It was FABULOUS! In spite of the long queues and aching feet. He was a knock-out, from the moment he appeared on stage, the audience yelled and clapped their enthusiasm, from a 16-year-old in front to a very vocal New Yorker of about sixty at the back, they went wild.

Barry was dressed in black satin trousers and shirt, with a sequined top and started off with a grey/blue velvet jacket which he discarded after the first couple of numbers.

At the end, bunches of flowers were flung on stage. Jane commented in *Prelude*:

We sat there as drained and emotionally exhausted as he must have been, feeling we had participated together in this experience. I have never seen anyone like it – Barry must be THE performer of all time.

November 1980 saw the man himself back in Britain. At London's Heathrow airport the fans were out in force to give a mighty welcome to the one who has meant so much to them. Mollie and Lynn of the British Barry Manilow Fan Club had many a question buzzing through their heads as they and others raced towards Heathrow.

The distance suddenly seemed endless. They wondered whether other club members would turn up. They worried over whether Concorde might be delayed and even diverted or, at worst, simply cancelled. And then there was the question of parking. The whole event seemed fraught with difficulties and perils which had previously seemed incidental or irrelevant and had not even been entertained as threats. They made Heathrow without incident and then the company quickly poured out of their cars, producing an assortment of welcome cards, flowers, the vital cameras. These were clutched tight as they headed for the important arrival board to find details of landing.

There were cheers when it was announced that Concorde had landed. And suddenly there he was. The big moment had come.

Our Barry. He looked beautiful in casual shirt and jeans, carrying a large floppy hat, and wearing a fabulous grey fur jacket. He was tanned and sensational. He looked very surprised to see such a crowd, genuinely delighted to know we were all there to welcome him, and slightly bemused by the whole thing.

'Welcome to London, Barry,' we said.

'What's that?' he replied, looking at the large disc we were waiting to present him with. As he came closer to examine it, he said, 'That's beautiful, but can I fetch it later?' and laughed. 'It will be collected later,' said one of Barry's companions.

Cameras flashed, endless flowers, teddy bears, letters and cards came his way. The passionate crowd surged forward, carried by its own momentum, then suddenly he was in a car and away into the night. It was the start of his two week visit. So wrote Hilary Porter expressing the feelings of all those who were there. Barry's fortnight in Britain had begun.

For countless thousands the Wembley Arena was the centre of the excitement. A hundred years would seemingly drag by for those who arrived at the concerts with irrational thoughts flooding their minds that perhaps their tickets were forged, perhaps they had come on the wrong evening, maybe the dates had been altered, that *he* might fall ill, that the lights and sound system might give out and ... just about anything which would cause chaos and upset was envisaged. It was alarming but natural, to be misunderstood by the unknowing but certainly a familiar name to those who regarded the evening as the highlight of the year, the past two years and for new fans perhaps even of a lifetime. Of course he would be there but ... all the same!

Anne McDonald of Northolt, Middlesex said:

Once through the turnstile I breathed a sigh of relief, happy to be able to dismiss earlier nightmares of losing the tickets, breaking down en route or getting cut off by snow, fire or floods! Barry, I thought, HERE I COME.

The climb up to our seats was a long one and I half-expected to end up outside on the roof! But no, they were – empty too, thank goodness. (That was another nightmare – a double booking!)

Eventually, though, her hero was on stage, wonderful moments were hers, the applause sounded sweet, the magic of Barry Manilow was evident. And at the end?

When it was all over and the magical white figure disappeared into darkness for the last time I felt no trace of the sadness I'd expected to feel at the end after all those long months of waiting. Apart from wet eyelashes, a finger-smeared programme and a used candle there was nothing tangible left – just an overwhelming joy in my heart and the memory of a night I shall never forget.

Dorothy Younger found that for days after the concert she was unable to speak sense to anyone.

I was absolutely emotionally drained for two days, to hear those beautiful songs sung with so much feeling and depth, and all performed so superbly.

Barbra Dean said that when the lights dimmed, thousands of hearts beat faster, and then:

Oh, my God – there he was! Black pants, shirt and white jacket! This must be Utopia! This is the promised land! A year's membership, four months' wait for tickets, my family driven insane by Barry who? And here he was and here was I! The next few hours sped by. Tears in my eyes, pain in my heart, hands sore from clapping, feet tired from stomping, bottom sore from jumping around!

Similar sentiments were expressed by Carolyn Owen who felt that she was a lucky one amongst the mass of 8,000 people at Wembley on a November evening:

I was caught up in a feeling of excitement that was transmitted from each and every individual in that vast place. Their hero was about to step onto the stage ... I felt the awe of the audience as his voice resounded throughout the vast arena which had seen football matches, boxing, tennis tournaments – but never anything like the atmosphere which enveloped that small corner of London that evening.

These expressions of sheer pleasure found their way into *Prelude* 4.

Once the Wembley concerts were over some British fans were determined to catch Barry in concert again. On 13 April 1981 they flew to Las Vegas on a trip arranged in conjunction with the British daily newspaper, the *Daily Mirror*.

Mollie and Lynn of the British Barry Manilow Fan Club hoped to present Barry with a special souvenir book of his UK concerts. They did give Barry the book, but the fans also received some bad news. Barry's proposed return visit to Britain in 1981 had been postponed until the following year.

But at least Barry's new TV show went ahead as planned. His shows have given the devoted fan a most welcome chance to see Barry.

Two of Barry's major US TV shows have already been mentioned, those of 2 March 1977, 24 February 1978, both from ABC-TV. The third, once more by the ABC

company, was aired 23 May 1979. It was simply and aptly
called *The Third Barry Manilow Special. Billboard*'s review had
the caption 'Manilow's Latest Special Knocks on Emmy's
Door'.

It was produced by Barry and Ernest Chambers and the
guest star was John Denver. It was a nine-song show,
intimate and personal, opening with shots of Barry as a
celebrity driving school student! 'Ready To Take A
Chance Again' was the first song, then 'New England'
and a new slowish number, 'Why Don't We Try A Slow
Dance' which has piano backing. 'I Write The Songs' was
part of a seven-minute production number, later after the
John Denver spot there was the inevitable rendition of
'Copacabana', 'Even Now', 'Somewhere In The Night'
and the finale, 'Could It Be Magic' while Barry took his
bow in front of the studio audience.

Denver's role was to sing 'What's On Your Mind' and
then to join Barry for a brief musical journey through hits
of the Everly Brothers including 'Bye Bye Love', 'Cathy's
Clown', 'Bird Dog', 'Wake Up Little Suzie' and the
plaintive lulling 'Dream'.

John J. O'Connor of the *New York Times* described Barry
as a genuine phenomenon on the pop music scene. He
saw pop and rock in constant flux, but there was nothing
temporary about Barry.

He seemed fascinated by the 'white set' and said:

[The set] consists of steps ascending either to infinity or
nowhere, depending on individual perceptions. Mr
Manilow appears at the top in a white-and-silver-
sequined costume that suggests he may be about to
offer several choruses of 'Rhinestone Cowboy'. But he
descends the stairs singing one of his own hits, pausing
occasionally to wiggle his hips self-consciously, which
triggers squeals of hysteria from his young fans.

He saw in Barry someone boyish, affable and genuinely

pleasant with a gently self-depreciating sense of humour and these ingredients had been packaged with skill into a television special. It was a TV hit. As with the previous two shows millions watched and heard their country's superstar.

In Britain, to the delight of fans, the Wembley concert was recorded for BBC TV. The producer Stewart Morris commented: 'He's exactly as he appears on stage, but what is exceptional about him is that he knows a lot about television. We now have some of the best television of Barry outside the US.' And certainly among the British press' TV reviewers the affair was received with warm praise. Patrick O'Neill of the *Daily Mail* said he was someone who had a particular aversion to televised rock concerts. They were usually badly lit, had poor sound and rarely captured the general atmosphere of the occasion. The Manilow affair was different. Technically, he felt, the TV version of this show was better than other televised shows he had seen and he thought some of this success was due to the personality of the American star.

> He has a special quality all his own – the Yiddish word for it is 'chutzpah' – a very special, cheeky quality that comes from having a big city education and living on your wits.
>
> Manilow has it in abundance.

Also televised for British TV were concerts from the Royal Albert Hall which took place during Barry's 1978 visit.

Writer Mick Brown, assessing Manilow's rise to the top in *Radio Times*, talked of Barry bridging the generation gap with a facility few contemporary performers could copy.

He found Barry far from gauche in person: 'tall, angular and expensively dressed, he exudes a self-assurance, which critical brickbats – English critics have likened him to everything from a "peroxide parrot" to "a

73

marionette in a corset" – have tempered with an understandable wariness.'

The TV show was watched by millions and the BBC was immediately engulfed in praise mail and endless requests for repeats. Of course British fans have watched the show and the Wembley concert countless times on video. Sometimes friends arrive from all over the country for impromptu playback sessions. For them there can never be enough of Barry live. And British fans are always at a disadvantage simply because the artist is American. A fourth special, *One Voice*, with guest star Dionne Warwick was screened during 1980.

Barry has carefully avoided over-exposure whether stage or television. Stage is less susceptible simply because the artist can be continually on the move and his audiences will differ from place to place. It takes a very long tour and constant year-in and year-out repetition of the same show to achieve anything even remotely approaching saturation. Television is a different game. It reaches its tentacles everywhere and always for any artist there is the continual worry that if a TV show fails then people may well conclude the live show is no better and that the artist, hits or no hits, is over-rated or is merely the product of a hype machine. Television is merciless in portraying a performer, every wart is clearly shown, every mistake seemingly magnified. At a concert the fan is some distance from his idol. On television the artist is thrown into the living room and cameras at the event can zoom to within inches of the performer giving the viewer a close-up he would never hope to have at a live concert. Television by its very nature is a picture on small screen. The concert stage by comparison is large. Shapes and sizes, lighting and general sound effects can be considerably different at a 'live' concert than on the twenty-four-inch screen and of course there is no comparison with a live concert when it comes to the sound. More worrying than most things though is the simple equation – you see a show at home, so why go out and see it. Of course it is always hoped that the converse will be true, that if you see the show on TV, you will go and buy the music you have heard, that you will become a fan and that you will prefer in the end to join with thousands of others and make the live concert pilgrimage. So it is often to the artist's advantage to restrict the number of TV shows they make. Barry Manilow has done just this and perhaps in view of the personal swipes made by critics, it is for his good.

For most rock performers the transition from the 'live' stage show to the TV special recorded and made in the studio is never easy and few come out with credit. Barry Manilow is one artist who does know the difference between stage and studio, who does adapt his performance for each form of medium and is successful in each. While the artist has his critics there have been few writers who have suggested he does not know the in-and-outs of presenting a show. Usually the critics have congratulated him on his sheer professionalism.

Chicago journalist Richard Christiansen writes:

He is, of course, a shrewd merchandiser and a skilled salesman, but in his stage personality, at least, he is still able to convey to his adoring fans the essential performer's enthusiasm that delights in and derives energy from a crowd's response.

Audiences instinctively respond to this kind of pep-rally professionalism, and, having spent two-and-a-half hours with Manilow's glossy production they feel certain that they've had their money's worth.

In the world of entertainment, there is no surer way to success.

It would be a mistake though to assume from this that

anyone with a modicum of talent can achieve so-called success by possessing the right formula. There is still the necessary charisma which Manilow obviously has.

Barry himself has from time to time come out with some interesting observations on his approach to stage and concert – he told Mary Campbell of AP Newsfeatures soon after he had started performing live:

> The strangest part of the whole thing now isn't the hit records. It's being a top-draw name concert attraction, selling out because people want to come and see me perform live. I wouldn't say I'd never go back to being a piano player and arranger. I liked that role. But I must admit I'm getting very spoiled with this one.

Yet Barry has often said that live performances demand from him extra reserves of energy. He told Sue Reid of the *Sunday Telegraph Colour Magazine*: 'It's like blowing up a balloon, the highs are higher, the lows lower. It's a whole different extension of myself.'

He is proud and justifiably pleased at the friendly rapport he has with his audience. Some artists rarely communicate with an audience on a 'chat basis' and if they do it's often a deliberate ploy to increase the intensity of their act at a particular moment, as for instance when a singer or group requests the audience to clap along with the beat or sing some verses of a song while he points the microphone in their direction. To Barry Manilow it's second nature. At Milwaukee, in 1977, he told his audience:

> Don't freak out if I talk to you too much. I'd like you to get to know me.
>
> If you feel like clapping, clap on two and four, one and three is Lawrence Welk.

At this January concert one fan threw a bouquet of flowers in his direction. It landed beneath his piano. Barry said with a grin, 'That was very thoughtful, but you've got a lousy aim.'

Obviously he's an artist who in spite of a basic unease at performing acquires a sureness and confidence on stage. And, he told me, he has always believed in stressing this personal relationship with his audience yet his triumph on stage is, like most things, unpremeditated and unexpected.

Barry told Britain's Garth Pearce in New York about what he hopes his fans see in him:

I hope they are screaming because they like what they hear. Being a sex symbol is not very substantial, really. I think the audience react to the passion of the music because I do unveil emotions which most male artists fight shy of. The first time they screamed I was frantic to calm them down. Now, I take a deep breath and let them go crazy because they want to − but it's very difficult. I run through the whole gamut of emotions while I'm standing there. Do I look like an egomaniac?

Once my life wasn't planned but now I even know what I may be doing two years' time. I meant it wasn't long ago when I didn't know what was happening at the end of a week. It's interesting having your life planned but at the same time it can leave you feeling you have no independence.

I guess freedom means not having to go on tour or give concerts when I don't want to. Right now there's no way I can take time off.

Barry has various theories on why he has been successful in numerous fields. His modesty affects what he says. He talks of the music scene being ready for an artist of his type. He says there is always a demand for a ballad singer, for someone with romantic lyrics.

For a time he felt he was slave to the very things he loved:

I discovered that all that frantic energy can work against you. It was at the time of 'I Write The Songs' when I suddenly realised how unbalanced my life was.

The most important things in my life were the No. 1 record, the sell-out tour, the television special. They all became more important than me as a person. And that's very foolish ...

I suddenly realised that I hadn't touched a piano for pleasure for a whole year. It wasn't fun anymore.

My whole life was devoted to music, just as I'd always wanted it to be. But it was for the wrong reasons.

I wasn't rushing into the studios because I had a great new idea for a song. I went because I had to produce the next single.

Now he feels he has put his career into the right perspective. He is aware that he is his own best asset.

Barry often says 'I am open for any suggestion' when journalists ask whether he contemplates widening his media activities into, for instance, the world of film. In the last few years he has been taking acting lessons from Nina Foch in Los Angeles. He says: 'It started off as a lark, now I don't know how I've lived without it. I'm going back to school with a group of other struggling young actors and I get up and make a fool of myself just like they do.'

He has hired a lady by the name of Sue Mengers for the purpose of finding him a good film script. He says: 'She is like a superagent. Her speciality is movies.' He told me: 'Nobody offers anything much, they give me crap. I have my acting lessons and I'm trying out my acting abilities. If I do a film it's got to be the right one.'

And Barry commented on TV appearances: 'If I decided to do a weekly series, I'm sure the record (sales) would go straight down the tube.'

IT'S MORE THAN PLEASANT HAVING BRITISH FRIENDS

'Management is so important. So is a good record company. Barry has both. And I like to think someone like myself, a DJ, is contributory toward his success.'

The speaker is David Hamilton, a genial and friendly British DJ who is known affectionately to millions of his radio listeners as 'Diddy David'. For all Barry Manilow fans he is simply a 'real friend'.

David is known as the jock who plays Barry's records most days of the week. He is rewarded by a veritable mountain of mail and the adoring attentions of grateful Barry fans wherever he travels.

He's been broadcasting for many years. He has worked for British Armed Forces Broadcasting in Germany. He has been a highly successful television announcer in the north-east of England. He became the straight man for leading British comedian Ken Dodd in *Doddy's Music Box*. It was through his work with Ken that he acquired the term 'Diddy'. In the early part of the 1970s David deputised for many British name DJs and eventually all his hard work and undoubted professionalism paid off. In 1973 he was given his own show between two and five in the afternoon. It was a chance he expertly took and he was well to the fore in the top ratings figures.

Radio One is more rock orientated than Radio Two but

it does give airtime to melodic and tuneful music.

David is extremely knowledgeable when it comes to class MOR music. It was quite obvious that he was a DJ who would play and enjoy spinning the records of the American super-star Barry Manilow. The fans thought this and they fairly wore their hands out writing requests. Diddy was only too happy to oblige. He believed that Barry had a unique talent and was someone who deserved a great deal of time on the airwaves, a view which did not appear to be universally held, judging from other radio shows on Radio One and Radio Two.

'I think I can honestly say I was "in there" at the start. Initially there was very little reaction to Barry in the UK. It was the classic example of a talented artist, a very energetic record company and people like myself saying how good he was, and not too much interest from the general record buying public. It seemed ages before he really got moving. I helped things along with a Bank Holiday Special which was repeated a few times. I interviewed Barry especially for this.'

David had one special feature on his daily show. It was called 'Hot Shot' – each day of a respective week the same record was featured and listeners were told that this particular disc should be a hit. One disc he featured was 'Mandy'. Later when a major compilation record company, Warwick Records, issued an album entitled *David's Hit Shots*, 'Mandy' was one of the chosen record tracks.

'Mandy' was a British hit in 1975 and it was a long time before the follow-up hit, 'Can't Smile Without You', in 1978. 'It was strange really, that long gap. In some ways, odd as it may sound, record sales are not always synonymous with an artist's popularity, though of course sales are most important where finance is concerned. I think Barry is the top of his type. America is different from the UK. There they have great respect for singer-

Barry with his dog, Bagel

Bette Midler, who gave Barry his big break

Lynette Bennett and Dionne Warwick, two artists whom Barry has successfully produced

Above: Barry in concert, 1980 (David Redfern)

Top Right: Barry playing the accordian, an instrument he learned at 7 (John Everist)

Bottom Right: Barry arriving at Heathrow for his 1980 tour (Denise Robinson)

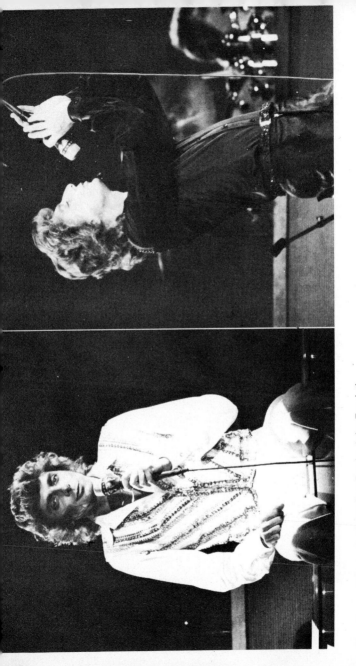

Four faces of Barry on stage (Roy Davis, John Everist)

Top: Barry with Radio Hallam DJ Keith Skues
Bottom: Barry with Molly and Lynn of the British Barry Manilow Fan Club
(Garry Kies)

songwriters and class performers. I think their chart is more adult-orientated. Sometimes in Britain there are those who think the "chart" is the sole guide to an artist. It's not always so. Barry, of course, after 1978 did do well in our British charts.'

David feels Britain has no ready-made market for MOR music even though there is a tremendous following and interest. He feels the audience is growing fast. 'In the UK Radio Two has overtaken Radio One. The latter will of course play some artists I and others would spin on Two. There are always crossover artists, someone for instance like Diana Ross. I don't think though you will find Barry played on Radio One.'

David thinks a DJ should be receptive to the needs of the listening audience. He also knows that as a DJ it's axiomatic that he should become involved with a particular artist.

'After my Special with Barry the mail poured in and it continues that way. When he has a new single I play it. When there is no single then I play album tracks. It would be crazy for me not to do this. So many people just want to hear Barry. I think if people want to hear certain artists then they should be given the chance to hear them.

'I was at the 1981 Barry Manilow Fan Club Convention. I was knocked out by it. I felt a tremendous warmth directed toward me. I felt I was basking in reflected glory. They were such a nice crowd, for the want of a better description! They were genuinely crazy about this man's music.

'As I said, I quite happily basked in someone else's glory. I think this country is crying out for artists of Barry's type.'

David, of course, works very closely with his producer on BBC Radio Two. 'Geoff Mullins has his finger on the button. Really does. I think of all Barry's tracks the one I enjoyed the most is "Even Now", that's lovely. I've got quite a kick out of helping Barry to be heard. I've always enjoyed this aspect of my job. I remember how I did my part in making the Philadelphia sound popular along with another fine producer, Paul Williams. And then there was The Three Degrees. I was down for some announcing duties for the show *Sunday Night At The Palladium*. The star should have been Clodagh Rodgers, but she was unwell. The Three Degrees stepped in. I was really knocked out by them. They had this song entitled "Year of Decision". I said to my producer that we must play the record. We did. It was a big hit and the girls were away into big-time.

'I'm genuinely pleased that I've played my part, such a good feeling you get from it. The guy is a splendid person. I enjoyed meeting him. He was perfect for interviewing. He had so much to say, ten sentences for every question. Amazing! He was quite a contrast from some stars I could name who can hardly put together more than a few sentences! He's a super-star and deservedly so.'

'Diddy' David Hamilton may be a major proponent of the Manilow magic but he's not the only one. Listeners in South Yorkshire realised on Easter Monday, if they had not known before, that the programme director of Radio Hallam and sometime station DJ, Keith Skues, had an enthusiasm for the American's music.

Skues put together interview material and records to produce a two-hour special between 10.00 a.m. and 12.00 noon under the title of *Manilow Magic*. Skues is known worldwide for his work with Tim Blackmore at that time an executive BBC producer on the Radio One series *Story Of Pop*. He spent many years working for British Forces Broadcasting Service and broadcasting as a DJ with Radio One and Radio Two. So his choice of a Manilow special came from a background awareness of good music and popular appeal.

He kindly gave me a copy of the interview he had with

Barry and I repeat it here because it makes interesting reading and also shows Barry's fans and the merely curious the kind of interview the American gives.

Keith: Barry, the first time we as a radio station came to know of your name was back in the latter end of 1974, when Hallam first went on the air. A record called 'Mandy' was a new release, and indeed a record which we, from our playlist, broadcast regularly. Meanwhile back in America, you'd put quite a lot of hard work into the music business before the big break. You were born in Brooklyn, New York in 1946 and from that day onwards you were surrounded by music.

Barry: I come from a poor family, but I was happy, and so was my family. High school was interesting, but nothing special. There was always music in my family, and in my life, but I never really considered making music as a living. It never really dawned on me that I could make a living or a career in music, and coming from a poor background the most important thing is that Friday afternoon payslip. You really need the rent money. And so, when I graduated from high school, my parents said, 'go get a job', and I did. I worked in a few jobs. But there was always music. I was always playing the piano for somebody, or playing in a nightclub. I also got married, and I was being promoted to a junior executive. Everything seemed to be going pretty normally, but the music just seemed to be taking over, so I then decided to give it a shot. I was divorced, and left New York, and I went to pursue my musical wild notes, which I have never regretted.

Keith: How did you find time to attend the New York College of Music?

Barry: I could not afford to go to college full-time so I would work in the afternoon, go to music college in the evening, and then play with a band or in a show at night to make some money. It was a very wild and energetic life I was living.

Keith: Did you have to pay for your own tuition?

Barry: I had to pay for my own everything! At the end of high school, my parents told me to go. I had to pay towards the rent, and also for my living. I decided to go to school on my own, and so I had to pay for it.

Keith: How did you first get involved in the record industry?

Barry: I was working as a mail boy for CBS. I was then promoted, and was doing pretty well as an executive. But, I decided to leave that normal way of life and pursue music as a career. The first things I did were to accompany singers, sing in night-clubs, and also in Broadway plays. Most of all I was making a healthy living coaching singers, playing the piano and doing arrangements for singers. One of the singers that I worked for was Bette Midler. We had a nice time and started each other off on the road. I was her conductor and musical director, and also her record producer. It was a wonderful collaboration, and the year she went off on vacation was the year I decided to try and make a record of my own. I made some demonstration records, and Bell Records bought me as a singer. But they said they would not do this unless I promised to go out on the road myself and perform in front of the public. I did this and it worked.

Keith: Before you became involved with Bette Midler, you were involved with a Broadway production called *The Drunkard.* After that, you were called on to television, you were involved in a production called *Callback*, and you also worked for Ed Sullivan, I believe?

Barry: Yes, it all seemed to be happening for me at the same time. I was learning and getting a lot of experience. I made a lot of commercials and jingles. I learnt about recording techniques and writing songs in general.

I was already on tour before the first hit record. I worked in the major cities, Chicago, Philadelphia, Los Angeles and Washington. In the year that Bette took off, I made an album, and then I went back with Bette for a short time. I opened her second act with three songs of my own, which was like the Suicide Spot. Bette would come off the stage after her first act, having the audience in the palm of her hand, and as I was conducting her last song, I would know that after the intermission I was going to come out unbilled, unannounced and try and sing three songs they had never heard before, and they wanted to see Bette. It was never uncomfortable, her audience were always very nice to me. They would even stand after I sang 'Could It Be Magic'.

This is the total opposite to the type of song that Bette would sing. They never threw the tomatoes I had expected! This encouraged me to go on my own. The next time out was on my own. I then went back to doing small clubs. It was terrifying and I was terrible, but it was quite an experience. My audiences gradually got bigger and bigger, and then 'Mandy' had hit No. 1. But, unfortunately, I was bankrupt. You don't become rich on your first record. You have to pay the record company and the musicians. We managed to work our way back to New York, which was quite dramatic. I didn't write 'Mandy'. The original title of the song was 'Brandy'. Scott English and Richard Kerr wrote it. I didn't sing the word Brandy because there was already a record called 'Brandy' out, by Looking Glass, and we did not want it to have any confusion. So we just changed the title to 'Mandy'. I don't know why we came up with Mandy. We could have called it Sandy or any one of a million names. Mandy was a pretty sounding name.

Keith: You don't always write songs do you, so how do you choose your song writers?

Barry: Well not always, I sometimes write the words and

most of the time I write the music. My collaborators and I work together on the lyrics. Most of the time they give me wonderful lyrics that I try and put decent melodies to. There are many songs in my repertoire that I have not written myself. Other songwriters have written them which is just fine with me.

Keith: You would be described as melodic, tuneful, and most definitely memorable. But every so often you can change your style, especially on album tracks.

Barry: I think this is vital. As a matter of fact, I would love for my singles to have as much variance and diversity as my albums do. But the public seem to like the one style – the big ballad style. I do like to diversify my albums. So the albums are different, which is perhaps, I think, why they sell more than singles do.

Keith: It must be difficult for you, Barry, to identify with your stage shows, and then to come off stage and be Barry Manilow as yourself. How do you actually adjust to this kind of life?

Barry: This is the most difficult part of it. The loss of privacy is the most difficult thing to make peace with. But it's a small price to pay. The way I deal with it is, I try to deal with my life as normally as I can, in the midst of this crazy career. When I'm on the road, I'm very visible and public property. When I'm not on the road, I try and deal with my life as I would have done if this had not happened. I don't surround myself with bodyguards, or security people. I go shopping, I go to movies, I go to restaurants. I insist that I stay as normal as I possibly can. If people come up to me and ask me for my autograph, it's a small price to pay. So far, it has not really stopped me. I've got a lot of money now and I've got a lot of things. This is enjoyable, but it's not really where it's at for me. Where it's at for me, is to keep my feet on the ground and to keep doing what I've always done. I think I will always be able to make a living. The singing and entertaining part is enjoyable, although it is not life and death to me, and I hope it will always stay there. If it doesn't, I don't think I'll die. I'll probably be around for a while.

The latter is a statement Barry's fans would sincerely hope will be true!

Keith Skues also interviewed some of Barry's local fans for his *Manilow Magic* show. He spoke with Mandy Galloway from Westwoodside, near Doncaster. Mandy said she had met Barry at a London press reception and she found he was just 'absolutely terrific' and he was the opposite of what some people had told her. They had given the impression that he was a difficult man to talk to and that she would have to be terribly careful as to the kind of question she asked lest the star departed. 'Anyone who asked him a question was given the courtesy of a full answer and he didn't turn down any questions whilst we were there and he was talking about his girlfriend for the first time and why he has not married again, all the things we had been warned off, in fact.'

She told Keith Skues of how she had seen Barry in concert at Stafford's Bingley Hall. 'When he came on stage we could just make out this little black blob against a white piano and that was it. Once he started to play, however, it didn't matter how far back we were because he is such a fantastic showman that he held the audience of maybe 10,000 in the palm of his hand, every woman there just wished that she was the only one that he was singing to.'

Keith asked her how she would compare Barry to other artists who played similiar music. But, to Mandy, Barry was unique. And when she was asked whether he was unique because of the songs or the way he sings those songs she answered: 'It's got to be the way he sings them. Obviously the songs are important for he describes himself as the singer of thoughts not just melodies – the way he puts them over is pretty terrific.'

Mandy told Barry of an article she had read about him. In this feature it was said that he poured a ghastly concoction of honey and wheatgerm over his hair and drank another one because it soothed the cuticles. She asked him if all this was true. It seems he shook his head with horror and, 'his eyebrows disappeared somewhere behind his neck'. He denied it with some force. Keith asked her how he seemed as a person. He remarked how on stage he didn't seem shy while off stage he has the reputation, true or not, of being withdrawn. Mandy explained that as far as she can see: 'it's like being two different people. He has to get very wound up to go on stage and until recently I believe he was actually physically sick before performing, he hates it so much. It was the aspect of his career which I think he would probably have most liked to have dropped. But now he is much more relaxed about it ... So we say what does the other Barry Manilow do and he says, "Well, I'm just like everybody else, I eat, sleep and watch TV a lot." '

For his *Manilow Magic* show Keith landed one major scoop. He interviewed Dionne Warwick, an internationally respected artist, the hit singer of numbers like 'Anyone Who Had A Heart', 'Walk On By', and 'You'll Never Get To Heaven'. Barry has produced an album for Dionne. Keith asked her the simple basic question:

Keith: Dionne, when did you first meet Barry?
Dionne: I met up with Barry Manilow about five or six years ago (1974/5). I gave Barry his first job. He opened my show. He had just left Bette Midler where he conducted piano for her and decided he wanted to try it on his own and I gave him his first job ever as a single artist on my show at Central Park in New York. He was just an adorable child, he was just so thrilled with everything and

that was of course in conjunction with his great success as a jingle writer, as you call them, with the McDonalds commercial and the Pepsi generation and a few other responsible kind of things that made him quite a very, very wealthy young man at very tender age. And five years later, after he'd had a great amount of success, I was kind of thrown back into a relationship with Clive Davis and we discussed the fact that I belonged with the company, because that's what I grew up with. The company was like a family situation, in fact it was small primarily but it was a good company and they cared.

And I agreed with him and then he said, 'I have a producer for you.' After about four or five months of talking about who would produce me he mentioned Barry. I said, 'I love Barry, I adore him, I think he is a wonderful artist, but no.' And he said, 'Why not?' and I told him that I felt that Barry, being his own producer and songwriter, would find it a very difficult task to come outside of himself to produce Dionne Warwick and really I was not going to be the female copy of Barry Manilow.

And Clive said, 'Well let me talk to him because he is really high on the fact of the thought of producing for you.' And Barry requested that we sit down and have dinner and talk, and I did, and after about twenty minutes of him ranting and raving and carrying on saying he knew he could do and don't worry about this, I'm gonna wear my producer's hat etcetera. He was crazed, I was just so impressed with his enthusiasm that I said, 'OK we'll give it a try.' And as a result it was a very big success and I am as pleased for him as I am for myself.

Diddy Hamilton and Keith Skues have helped to further Barry's career in Britain. A good record company is also vital and UK Arista can take credit for their continued efforts to push Barry in Britain.

In 1979 Arista released *Manilow Magic* backed by a big PR

and advertising campaign.

One of the people responsible for the press campaign was Howard Harding, who was also publicist for the major 1981 British Barry Manilow Fan Club Convention.

These days he no longer works for Arista. He is now in charge of press and public relations for the major Bastable company. But he was thoroughly involved with Arista's press and promotional activities from the moment Manilow's name travelled the Atlantic.

Harding, tall, good-looking and known as one of the smartest PRs in the British music business, joined Arista in March, 1975. 'At that point "Mandy" was a massive hit and Barry was soon to become a consistent-selling artist in the US but not here. Oddly after the single triumphed there was nothing happening.

'I remember we all talked and talked this one. We concluded it was because he wasn't here. He was not associated with his records. People, I think, like to know a face, to feel they know the artist. We knew we were faced with a mighty problem. We wanted him in the UK but he was so big and busy in the States. The more he became huge there the less likely was our chance of persuading him to come over.

'Eventually he did come. The press came to a reception in droves, surprising in some ways, outwardly there was nothing much happening for Barry in the UK and yet there was obviously support amongst writers and others.

'I remember the first personal meeting with Barry. He came into the office late in the day, I thought he was rather nervous, shy in a way. He was unlike the typical star. I think he felt uneasy, rather awkward, for he was meeting droves of people who knew little of him and yet 6,000 miles away everyone knew whether they liked his music or not.

'It was difficult for him. I mean when he came here he was having to explain who he was. It was ridiculous when you think of it. It must have been really strange for him.

'I think overall my strongest impression of him is how he was willing to sit down and discuss with us the things we were trying to do for him.

'And for us as a record company he was good. Record people tend to work in set formulas. The personnel sit down at weekly meetings and they map out familiar-style programmes. With Barry it was something which could not be done. You just couldn't pigeon-hole him. This artist seemed unique, an original talent. Quality.

'I think he has a fantastic voice, he's a brilliant arranger, and he has limitless possibilities, but I remember thinking then, how do you get all these things across? He has a magical quality. 45s have never been his strong point in this country whereas the albums have really sold.

'He came in 1978 and the amazing thing was that we didn't have to tell everyone about it by means of an expensive campaign, because his six shows sold out within hours. He arrived and he had full house signs up. Obviously he had an audience, but no one really knew he was so popular. I think it made many in the media sit up and take notice.

'It took a long time for the buzz about Barry to grow. From 1978, though, it was different. The floodgates opened and you found there were fanatical and fervent Barry followings all over Britain.

'I remember it took some persuasion to set up the Palladium dates. I think his management and doubtless Barry as well wondered what would happen if he came and no one bought any tickets. It was a real fear and you could find evidence to support it. If he had come and found a disaster and then read the ensuing press reports of his UK rejection then it would have depressed him and affected his career.

'From the moment he opened at the Palladium,

though, you just knew it was success all the way. The press, save for a small few, raved with enthusiasm.

'I remember everything had to be very well organised – professionalism and the highest standards are everywhere in the Manilow camp. There was extensive checking of who should interview Barry and we ensured that those who did knew what they were talking about.

'I think Barry has had some unkind press and usually it's nothing to do with his music or act, just snide remarks about his nose or something. All a pity, really.

'He's a very American artist and somehow I feel certain parts of the UK press are not into taking the artist's music seriously. They tend to float around the surface. I think it will change. I think informative material will come. I think people want it.'

Barry's friends in the media have made major contributions to his success in the UK, but even more vital are his fans.

YOU NEED FANS

It was cup final Saturday. The day was overcast. Every now and then it rained. The Wembley Stadium resounded from the roars of football fans. Millions across the world watched the game thanks to the marvels of satellite.

Some miles away on the south side of London another event was taking place and it was attended by fans just as devoted as the football addicts.

This latter occasion was at the Queen's Hotel, Crystal Palace. It was the first national convention of the British Barry Manilow Fan Club. Some 600 members had journeyed from all corners of Britain, as far afield as Cornwall and Stirlingshire, and had arrived hours before the day's programme commenced at 11.00 a.m. They stayed until midnight. It was a day for Manilow addicts. The events included screenings of all major US, UK and European TV spectaculars that the artist has recorded over the years. It had been claimed that this would be the first time that such a comprehensive mix of Manilow movies had been shown at one time under one roof. There was also an extensive range of Manilow memorabilia, too, available for fans to examine or buy.

The various hotel rooms which were utilised by the fan club rang continuously without a moment's pause with Barry's music. There was even a Barry Manilow disc-jockey and several singers who had written songs in Barry's style. Among the guests at the top table for dinner were leading MOR disc-jockey David Hamilton, Barry's British tour promoter Andrew Miller, songwriter Geoff Morrow, who wrote Barry's massive worldwide hit 'Can't Smile Without You', and singer-songwriter Gerard Kenny who penned 'Made It Through The Rain' and 'Nickles And Dimes'. Each was greeted with considerable enthusiasm and each spoke to the gathering of their respect for Barry and their involvement in his illustrious show-business career. There were special presentations for people judged to have contributed to Barry's success. DJ David Hamilton was one, another was Andrew Miller. Liverpool DJ Dave Lincoln, former Managing Director of Arista Records, Charles Levison, BBC TV producer Stewart Morris were the other recipients of awards.

Tears were shed during the day and two of those suitably overcome were two housewives, Mollie and Lynn. No one begrudged them their emotional moments for it was these two who had organised the event and who were the founders of the British Barry Manilow Fan Club.

A special recorded message from Barry was played to the 600-strong convention at the end of the dinner. In this message the American artist expressed how he was flattered by the day's activity and the club's general interest in his music. He said he was constantly amazed by what people did to further his career and he was especially grateful for the efforts of Mollie and Lynn. Manilow said: 'I have never seen people work harder, to work for me and bring my music to everybody.' He gave a big 'thank-you' as signing off the message which had been telephoned across the Atlantic and recorded the previous evening. It was a surprise ending to a day which saw an uninhibited display of what could only be called Barrymania.

Emma Soames, of London's *New Standard*, said that the

fervour at the Fan Club Convention was unbelievable. She learnt of fans who knit Barry sweaters, write him poems, travel to Las Vegas to see him and who, on this occasion, had paid £14.24 for the day's events.

Yet this particular day and the British Fan Club itself might never have been but for two things: Mollie and Lynn's sudden realisation that Barry Manilow is contemporary music's 'greatest', and their determined fight against attempted American domination and control of Manilow fan activity.

The two fan club organisers first saw Barry on British television. Their response was the same. This guy was the 'tops' in whatever category might be named. They saw Barry as someone bursting with talent: he came across as genuine, unaffected, and free from star arrogance.

'I think we felt he was totally unpretentious, level-headed. He was multi-talented. I hope he doesn't, but if he should give up performing or if, horrors upon horrors, his singing career collapsed, then there are so many other musical things he is good at. He can write great songs, he's an arranger, a producer, and he could be a major film star.

'I think performing is the aspect of his career he least enjoys but he does play live concerts because he feels he owes this to the people who buy his records. We saw Barry in Las Vegas and we thought how uncomplicated it all was. He didn't wear endless rings and sequins.

'We remember him when he performed in London. He was so natural. Some of those who came did so in their Rolls Royce cars and extravagant clothes, minks and diamonds. He wasn't into that kind of thing.'

Mollie and Lynn remember their first personal meeting with Barry. Again they recognised that he had no 'airs and graces' but was someone clearly touched by their appreciation and confidence in his musical ability.

They told me:

'We had been asked to meet the concert's promoter, Andrew Miller. We met him at the box office after the Friday concert, and assumed it was something to do with tickets. When Andrew began to escort us towards the back-stage area, panic began to set in!

'He still didn't tell us where he was taking us, but when we were actually behind the stage and were told to sit on a packing case and not to move and because it was so secretive we did begin to think perhaps Barry was involved in some way.

'It was not until we were actually in Barry's dressing room, and he came over to meet us, that it finally dawned on us what was happening.

'Can you imagine the feelings that were racing through our minds right then? Here before us was *Barry* – the reason for everything that our lives revolve around. Here was *Barry* – whose music means so much to us, and to all our friends out there, who we were representing.

'I mean here was *Barry* – the man we had come to know and love over the past two years. And here he was saying to us, "Hello – it's nice to meet you. You're doing a great job with the fan club." Well, it was just too much, and we were almost overcome by the whole thing.

'I think we had worried unnecessarily. Barry made us feel completely at home, and we managed to pull ourselves together and started to talk to him.'

The two remember how they felt nervous and even physically sick because of the greatness of the occasion. Then they recall how he made them feel at ease and above all made them feel that they were welcome even though he must have been tired and emotionally drained after his concert performance.

'He asked us if we were enjoying the concerts, and said that surely we didn't intend going again the next night to listen to his cornball jokes. We said, 'Try and keep us away!'

'At this point Barry kindly introduced us to Roberta Kent, saying she was a very good friend of his, who helped him with his stage act, which included the jokes.

'Roberta said hello and laughingly said, "I do the cornball jokes, Barry is responsible for the good ones," and at this Barry gave out a chuckle and laugh, and said, "That's not true."

'We then asked Barry if he was enjoying his visit to Britain this time, and whether he was pleased with the concerts. He replied: "Oh, yes, it's incredible, I've never felt such warmth from an audience before, it's fantastic, and what a lovely welcome I had at the airport."'

Mollie and Lynn met Barry during his autumn concerts in 1980. Although it was hardly the Christmas season it was equally the real opportunity to present him with a special Christmas present from the fan club. They gave him a resplendent yet tasteful decanter.

'He protested at the gift but words could not describe the look on his face when he saw it. He said something like "That's just beautiful" and he asked how we had obtained it. We told him of a very skilled craftsman who lived in Scotland and who had very kindly made it for us.'

The decanter had one particularly precious aspect for Barry. When it was held to the light it clearly showed a dog's face, a striking likeness to his own precious Bagel. The two ladies recall Barry's words:

'That's just what you need – after being away from her for six months. It's a beautiful present.'

Mollie and Lynn later described their meeting with Barry for their thousands of fan club members.

In their fan club newsletter they wrote:

The thing we can share with you all is that he is exactly how he appears on stage, warm, kind, sincere, completely unaffected by stardom. He is so natural. He laughs the same, talks the same, and his facial expressions are the same. His humour and radiant, warm personality are very noticeable, but at the same time he has a humble shyness that makes you think he is in awe of everything around him, as if it's happening to somebody else. Don't believe the things the critics say (not that you do anyway), they are not giving a fair account of Barry. In fact, after meeting him, we are convinced there must be a lot of journalists who qualify for a disability allowance – due mainly to the fact that they can neither see or hear! Perhaps one day God will look on them kindly, and restore their faculties. When that day comes, they will then be able to see and hear Barry the way we do, and with that gift comes Manilove, which will make them much nicer people. Until that day, we must sympathize with them, for what is lacking in their lives.

Mollie and Lynn also remember their former affection for Frank Sinatra. They saw this long-time idol on stage in London. Sinatra on this occasion sang a Barry Manilow song and he told the audience that if they had the chance of seeing this American performer live then they should for he was very talented. The two took one of the world's greatest singers and performers at his word and did just that. Sadly, it might seem, for Sinatra, he's now been relegated to number two. The Manilow man leads the field. As the two told me: 'Look at us now!'

The two have seen the fan club grow and grow during its short two-year life. There was a Barry Manilow Fan Club before Mollie and Lynn thought of starting one but it made little impact and the two girls longed for a club which would really spread the Manilow message. They talked with the existing organiser and they had conversations with both British and American personages who were involved with the various aspects of Barry's career. The response appeared positive and Mollie and

Lynn began establishing a really alive and vibrant Barry Manilow Fan Club. However early joy at receiving an immediate response of 800 applications was tempered and dulled by some frantic communications which came winging their way across the Atlantic. The American side of Barry's organisation decided things were not right.

Mollie and Lynn told their members:

We are writing this from the padded cell! After we explained to the doctor that the fan club must operate whatever, they allowed us to share one, and provided a typewriter. Seriously, it nearly came to that! Boy, have we had some problems, but all's well that ends well. The trouble began when the American side of Barry's organisation decided they wanted to *take us over*. Cheek! We were determined not to go down without a fight, and battle commenced. It raged furiously for a couple of weeks with us refusing to budge. We knew from those of you whom we had managed to hurriedly contact that everyone wanted to keep the *British* Fan Club *British*, and not be swallowed up into a huge international complex which would operate from California. Well, we don't quite know how, but we won! We prepared a newsletter informing you of these plans and asking for your views and support if you agreed with what we were doing.

The very day we picked it up from our deranged printer (who is now sharing the same cell!!), we had a call to say, OK, you win, but on a certain condition. This condition is that we agree to pass over to the international organisation all names and addresses of the British Fan Club members. You will therefore be hearing from them, and of course, it's your choice whether you decide to join.

Mollie and Lynn supplied the list. Some of the British Fan Club do belong with the international organisation but little has come from that quarter in comparison with the hectic activity of the British Fan Club.

August 6, 1979 was the magical day when the British Fan Club was born. It had 8,000 plus members within two years. At Mollie's house the two nationally known housewives told me: 'It was pretty terrible at the time – on our nerves! I can remember the call – they said there was terrible news for us. We were determined however. We felt they did not really understand things over in the States. We merely wanted things done the right way for Barry. He does need so much support in Britain. And we wanted to help in every way possible.

'I remember we took legal advice. The solicitor was dumbstruck. I don't think he had ever encountered this kind of problem before! British people are not an easy touch for the Americans! We were told that there was nothing they could do on the legal front because in fact we had started up before the Americans and we could even have claimed copyright on the name. We just dug our heels in and of course we were spending our hard-earned money to do this.'

The two ladies talk with fascinating zeal and ardour. Their dream which may well become reality is simple – that British airwaves and households resound to Manilow. They are grateful for the artist's appreciation of their efforts to establish him in the UK as the undoubted superstar he is in the United States. Naturally they are pleased that there is now good relations with the Stateside Manilow camp.

Manilow fans come from all parts of the age spectrum. The youngest fan club member is not yet in her teens and the oldest is over seventy. They share with Mollie and Lynn this extraordinary enthusiasm and in addition to expressing their love for the artist many of those who wrote to me expressed how much they appreciated their being such an excellent British fan club.

The letters which came my way were not solicited through the fan club. They came because I attended the British Barry Manilow Fan Club Convention that May afternoon in 1981 .

Joy Kübler of Eccles, Manchester explained how her love for Barry was on a different plane than, say, her love for her husband and children.

She wrote:

When I'm listening to him I believe he's singing every word for me personally. He sings songs that can make me cry and then come back for more. He comes over as a most sincere and genuine person. He cares for his fans and also for the people who work for him …

Mandy Loring is of the new pop generation: she is 16. She enjoys current pop music but finds Barry 'special' and 'very sexy and extremely sensual'. She is attracted by his warm, friendly personality, and by the way he speaks to concert audiences as if they are all his personal friends, who he has known for years. 'He is a self-confessed romantic: not as some people say, a hopeless romantic, but in his own words, a hopeful romantic. All his fans are very romantic people, and have very deep emotions. He sings every song very emotionally.'

Many of those who wrote explained that their husbands think they're 'nuts' for spending so much time involved with the American artist. Jacquie Humphries of Cardiff states that she is no love-struck teenager and if husbands and others fail to understand such enthusiasm it's because they cannot compete with the man. Janice Yates became a convert of Barry's after an evening babyminding left her with little else to do but watch television. On BBC 2 she saw a gorgeous, blond-haired man dancing with three women and singing one of the catchiest tunes she had heard for a long time. But it was a long time before she found out who this vision was!

Kim Phillips of Grimsby, who is twenty-one, is impressed with his sheer vocal ability and she feels he is an artist who enjoys the participation of his fans while he is singing. While her letter, in common with most, was short and straight-to-the-point, there were writers who analysed the Manilow magic at a deeper depth.

Margaret Croft of Manchester related Barry's comparatively poor upbringing and his early family instability with the kind of song and performance he gives.

Barry at the age of two was deserted by his father, never to experience the bond of love fathers and sons have. Despite this Barry has received all the love possible from his mother, who he fondly remembers as some kind of superhuman being. Perhaps these experiences have made Barry like he is today, as strong as he is.

People like Barry fight for what they want, they have something to believe in and they have a strong determination.

Margaret believes Barry is a very private person. She believes that as he grew up he experienced much loneliness. She sees him as someone who knew deep down inside himself that he could succeed in life and be whatever he wanted.

Barry's fans talk of him changing their lives in language more commonly used in religious circles. Some say they do nothing without thinking of him. Others simply agree with the sentiments of one letter: 'Without his music we are lost, we would have nothing in life to aim for,' and tell how depression and a general feeling of inadequacy have been overcome through knowing him, his music, and being part of an international movement of followers.

Letters express the writer's despair of life. For example:

I hated the place where we lived and worse still lost all

sense of purpose, there seemed to be no reason at all to go on living, no friends, no familiar surroundings, both my daughters getting married within a month and my husband wrapped up in his work, and being more isolated and farther away from civilisation than ever. There seemed no point in anything. I couldn't even cope with cooking or shopping, just walking out of shops without paying in the end.

Then Barry came along. His was the first show we recorded on video although we had never heard of him, and as soon as I saw it, he smashed his way into my life. Suddenly there was something to live for, not something easy: after a few months I went through hell wanting to meet him, talk about him, but being alone, not getting answers to letters, not seeing any way I could ever meet him. Still, it gave me something to live for, a purpose.

For this lady there was in the background a husband who took stock of the situation. She comments:

Fortunately my husband is constructive and resilient and saw it as a challenge, something which made me want to live again, so he backed me up and we went to California to take a pair of Minton statues as a present for Barry ... We've seen Barry in concert at Las Vegas three times and Lake Tahoe twice, then came Wembley and Bingley and finally four shows at Las Vegas's Riviera. It has certainly knocked a hole in our finances.

This writer, as others, tells of how the fan club has given them all new friends, of their own age and younger:

If I get fed up I can ring one of them up and have a natter and it dissipates the desolation of being completely alone.

Lesley Karen Barwood says: 'We're like one big happy family, and when we meet there's a bond between us all, we're like old friends and it's a marvellous feeling.'

Christine Richards of Blackburn was one of the fan club members who flew off to the States on a specially chartered flight and saw Barry perform in concert. She writes:

I was travelling alone and so my friends and family were understandably a little worried. They needn't have been, because as soon as I met up with the group at Gatwick I felt as though I had known them all my life. We had such a lot in common ... at the first concert, it was 8.00 p.m. and the lights went down in the theatre. The next minute there was Barry singing 'It's A Miracle' which summed up my feelings exactly.

One letter writer, Barbara Wells, from Stanmore, Middlesex, says she writes to Manilow fans all over the world. She was one of the 600 at the Crystal Palace Convention:

To see 600 people singing 'Who's Been Sleeping In My Bed' and 'It's A Miracle' on Saturday was unbelievable, but equally the sad songs are heartbreakers, as if he really has experienced every word he sings.

The emotions surrounding Barry are strange. I'm told that even he is baffled. Some people adore him. Few people can 'take him or leave him', they have to say really inaccurate, rude things, especially the critics from the press!

His music is described as 'middle-of-the-road' which I suppose is pretty untrue; the quality, however, is way above. They're not always his own lyrics or music but he somehow makes them sound like they are. Everyone has to be reminded for instance that Bruce Johnston wrote 'I Write The Songs'. Each song is different and yet alike in that he is the link ...

Mollie and Lynn are amazing people. I think the word is dedicated. It sounds corny but I would say that every woman at the convention is in love with Barry, including Mollie and Lynn!

Others see themselves gaining a much clearer sense of their own identity through their involvement with Barry and the fan club. Beverly Craze of Maidenhead claims:

Barry has made me a personality and even a small celebrity. Because of my love for Barry's music I have had a write-up in the *Hairdressers' Journal* (the trade Bible). I always have conversation with clients about Barry. They ask after him, tease me, cut pieces out of their paper for me. In fact I am known, which is no mean feat when you are an apprentice. I have been on Radio One (BBC national radio) answering questions on Barry, which had the clients ringing up with congratulations. All in all I have gained immensely from being a fan.

Faith Griffiths, a Welsh girl from Aberdare, mid-Glamorgan, is sixteen. She was born blind but various eye operations have given her her sight.

'It was a painstaking ordeal. Seventeen operations later, thanks to the skill of a brilliant surgeon, my sight is at its peak, and I'm happy ... As a teenager I've always felt very self-conscious about my eyes – I've lacked confidence and, in a nutshell, I used to consider myself unacceptable. I didn't used to go out because of my own stupidity, not because of others. Since I've known Barry, I have found that confidence, reassurance and joy which I have found can only be obtained from that extra special music ... I now enjoy a full life and am involved in any event concerning Barry – I think you'll agree when I say I owe Barry a great deal.

For Faith, for the many others who wrote to me, and seemingly for every Manilow fan, there is in the end no description which can do full justice to the way they feel. Margaret Davis puts it this way:

> Most singers or actors you like you go and see, and that's it, but Barry is special, you feel he is a part of you. It sounds stupid to someone who hasn't experienced it, but that's how it is.

The fans know Barry is grateful. One tangible form of their affection toward him is the presents they have given. One of the most spectacular was an inlaid backgammon set. Backgammon is Barry's favourite game. This set had a box made of solid mahogany, covered in French navy leather. The hinges and catches were finished in silver, and placed on the lid of the box was a solid silver plaque which had a special handgraven message: 'While you're away, we can't smile without you. Happy birthday 17th June 1980 – The British Fan Club.' The board itself had a teak background with inlaid cedarwood and rosewood markings, in the centre of each side of the board was a circle of ripple effect wood, with inlaid shadow writing in rosewood and cedarwood of the initials B and M. In one circle was the initial B and on the other side of the board in the second circle was the initial M. The counters had been made in solid cedarwood, with one set left in their natural state and the other set stained black. In the centre of each counter was a solid silver disc with the initial B engraved in the middle. The shaker cups for the dice had caused a slight problem. They were eventually made to measure and covered in matching leather.

Mollie and Lynn describe the whole thing as a work of art, and certainly a worthy gift for such a special person in the lives of the fan club members.

The fan club also supports the Jacques Cousteau Fund. This charity has received both commendation and practical help from Barry. Barry says he has received numerous requests for charitable endorsements and benefit performances but he has been particularly fascinated by the efforts of Captain Jacques Cousteau.

'As an ocean explorer for thirty years, he has dramatised the rapid deterioration of sea life. It is a disturbing situation caused by the same kind of human abuse that is destroying our land and air environment. His warnings, fortunately, are being heard.'

Barry Manilow gives as an example of the positive achievements of Cousteau: the Italian government's removal from the Mediterranean Sea of scores of drums of deadly gas from a sunken ship. The drums had been left to rust and disperse death through the waters for thousands of miles.

Barry says, 'The Cousteau Society is working to halt human destruction of the entire environment on behalf of future generations who cannot raise their voices against the degradation and consumption of their inheritance.'

In May 1981 the fan club received an unexpected accolade. The two fan club organisers were invited as guests to *Start The Week*, a long-running and high audience rated programme on BBC Radio Four. They talked not surprisingly of Barry, of their friends in the club, and of how he can lift a person to incredible emotional height, 'so that the adrenalin flows and you feel fresh as a daisy'. They described how they had met and talked with Barry. As they said: '6,000 of our members would stab us in the back for the privilege.'

Such is the passion of a fan club whose star is Barry Manilow.

THE VICTORY IS HIS

'Who do you write for?' says a rather suspicious-sounding
Barry Manilow. It's early evening. Barry is somewhere on
the American West Coast and I am in London. He follows
this with another question in which he basically enquires
as to the general tenor of the projected interview and
eventual newspaper article. He trusts I am not muck-
raking. He hopes I will not talk and centre my questions
on his personal life with his songs and music coming a
poor second.

He is reassured by my opening remarks, I mention I
know a friend of his from a long time back, Lynette
Bennett. It establishes between us an easy contact for we
have initial common ground. At first there is silence over
the transatlantic wires. He is thinking. And then he
remembers. 'Oh, yea, Lynette, wow, that is going back
some time, of course I know who you mean. Those were
great times we had. How is she? Where is she now?' And
from here our newspaper interview continues and I, the
reporter, know it will be a good one for the artist is at
ease. In any case I know of Barry's frequent tirades against
writers and, often, it would seem with justification, for he
has been vilified, the subject of cheap and nasty abuse and
usually at a level which is personalised. Rude remarks
have been made about his face and particularly the nose,

his so-called tinted blond hair, his incessant stage chatter, the knack of tripping over stage wires and the Hollywood stylised backcloths he apparently adores.

Manilow's hatchet critics have persisted with relentless zeal throughout his career and they show no sign of ceasing. There is little he can do right. And if it be true that all artists of any kind and nature suffer from adverse comments at some period in their careers it must be said that this Brooklyn singer-songwriter has had more than his fair share. Barry reacts either with disarming ease and simplicity, saying: 'These people don't consider me as a human being,' or, on occasion, spits out a whole bevy of words and lets loose his usually well controlled emotions.

'Critics, bah!' he once railed in 1977, 'What do they know? I was interviewed recently by a national rock magazine and finally came face to face with one of their critics. She had to be in her 60s, maybe more.

'Can you imagine a writer saying that my performance was "too clean cut"? What the hell did she want me to do, take my pants off on the stage? They all criticised my show at the Uris Theatre in December. But not one of them said that there were 4,000 screaming fans falling out of their seats. My two-week stand in New York was sold out two weeks in advance. Critics! I used to respect them until I realised the people I was being insulted by were people who knew much less than I do. I can't take them seriously.'

It's a battle in which Barry is supported by his fans. They are very conscious of their star being pilloried. Dianne Lowe is one young lady who both sees herself as a Manilow maniac and someone who none-the-less retains a sense of objectivity. She rages over the critics who tie Manilow into one bag and then hammer him.

Barry, on the evening of our conversation, makes a similar point. He says critics postulate that he is this and that and then having done so they busily begin their surgery. Meantime the real Barry Manilow cries for a hearing. At least he knows his fans are with him all the way and he would doubtless appreciate the sentiments of Britain's oldest fan club member, the mother of Sheila Reynolds, who calls him 'The Pied Piper' because she says he makes people follow him due to a combination of beautiful music and a marvellous personality.

Yet a Barry Manilow without the negative-sounding critics would be a strange creature. It all seems part and parcel of the major thrust in Barry Manilow's life-story, that here is a guy who relentlessly from early childhood never settled for less than what he believed was for him. He may have had doubts. He may have been faced with some awkward career decisions. He may have heard the advice of those who said he should stick at arranging music and aim no higher. Yet, in the end, it was the case of enormous self-belief which swept away everything which might have prevented the eventual stardom. And of course there is also the disarming way in which it was all achieved. Throughout his career Barry has time and time again protested that everything has come as if almost by surprise, undeserving and a mere bonus. To leave it at that would of course be to hide the artist's dedication, hard work and innate professionalism which has enabled him to take advantage of opportunities.

After all he does suggest he has the skill of the person who is too often in the right place at the right time, not just the luck. Take these examples: he found himself a job at CBS Records and it meant he made contact with people who contracted recording artists; he played initial secondary role to Bette Midler at the Continental Baths and it soon became apparent that he was technically qualified to arrange the musical scores on her first tour. When Bette hit the road it became obvious that a support act was needed and who better than Barry who was there on the spot. So the examples could continue. Manilow did spend years learning his craft; while others played games he practised his music. He became a skilled musician, arranger and producer and these are not attributes readily associated with most stars and most certainly not with the majority of people who populate the album and singles chart and who are here today and gone tomorrow. His success cannot be explained away with jibe and journalistic turn of phrase. 'Look, I love my job, it's the best job I ever had. We all like to get patted on the back.' And fortunately in the face of critical abuse he has retained a sense of humour which allows him to say, 'So far I've sold only fifty-seven records in Belgium,' and if the nasties dislike his facial profile then he himself can say: 'I was the ugliest kid in school. I never got a date. I had buck teeth and had to wear a brace. Big ears, a long nose and very skinny. I was a sight!' He also says: 'I'm working on my sanity!' And for all his stardom he is someone who can say: 'At this moment [1979] I don't even have a contract with my manager or agent. I work on a handshake.' It seems a refreshing change from the usual scenario of many a music star.

Barry, the singer who knows the victory is his, whatever the critics may say, comments: 'Yeah, I'm successful, yeah, I enjoy the success. I enjoy all of it. But the thing I work on most is keeping my feet on the ground in this hurricane. It's very difficult. The wind can knock you over.'

US NBC broadcaster Tom Snyder comments: 'He is the most unpretentious superstar I have met. I couldn't help but notice how he has matured since I first interviewed him on the *Tomorrow* show.' It's a comment far from the kind of remark which was made by British journalist Simon Kinnersley who has penned:

If Olivia Newton-John has cornered the nice-girl-next-door market then the male counterpart has been swept with great opportunism by the sincere Mr Manilow. He has become the Doris Day of the 80s ...

Obviously it depends on how you could define 'opportunism' but if the word is taken by its first dictionary definition – policy of basing one's conduct on present circumstances not on principles – then it seems an unjust assessment of the artist. Manilow is free from ruthless and sharp practice and the artist does not exhibit the lifestyle of someone who knows only one thing in life, sheer greed.

His manager Miles Lourie (who after all should know Barry better than most) suggests he is motivated by the refreshing drives of hard work, loyalty to those who prove their worth, and a basic trust in people. Lourie told *Record World*:

> One of the reasons I believe there is such a turnover in management and one of the reasons why managers are so vulnerable to dissatisfaction is that managers get very paranoid in keeping the artist advised of what's going on. Apart from Barry's inherent loyalty – I trust him implicitly – there have been occasions when other managers have approached Barry but nobody has ever been able to say to Barry, 'Do you know what Miles is doing?' without Barry knowing about it.
>
> If he doesn't know about it, it's not happening. It's really important. Most managers fail themselves by not keeping the act advised of what's happening. Because as soon as the act becomes successful, starts smelling success, they are vulnerable to somebody coming to them and saying, 'Do you know?' and the act saying, 'Oh, my God, I didn't know.' Trust disappears. The essential element is trust.

It all seems far from the world often postulated by critics. Manilow does not seem a big bad wolf, an unscrupulous scrambler after success, a fortunate over-rated singer-songwriter who lives in the land of clichéd music and banal lyrics aided and abetted by being wrapped in tinselled glamour, a colourless artist who exudes none of the aura of, say, a Rod Stewart or Sammy Davis Jnr.

If silicon and polystyrene are used liberally to remove blemishes and create the ideal figure, Manilow must be filled with the stuff from head to foot …

So writes Simon Kinnersley. And Manilow fans must grit their teeth, but if they pay too much attention they merely waste their energy. Manilow outlives any such critic although such people have every right not to like his voice, music, stage act and general presence. He survives simply because his success record is not the creation of a machine. He has been around too long to have succeeded just by hype but in any case analysis must – as this book has done – trace the artist back to his early days. In this artist's case the beginning, as the days following, tells of dedication and hard work. The critics snarl but Manilow knows the victory is his.

MANILOW MAGIC

The future is an open cheque for Barry. So many sides of his talent await development. Record fans yearn for further albums, more live appearances, endless magazine articles. Those in the business watch with interest his record producing which has already brought two much praised works with Dionne Warwick and Phyllis Hyman. Everyone looks for new ventures into musicals or the more likely field of film. Amazingly, Barry keeps his cool. He has learnt over the years the value of waiting for the right project and the apposite moment.

In one sense an open future might be regarded as ideal. Thousands of artists would give their right hand for the choice which Barry seemingly possesses. But for an artist of Manilow's calibre and public standing there is little room for mistakes and the more career possibilities he has at his disposal the higher the odds on his making a rash or false move. A star of his class cannot afford a bad album or a single which has low sales. There are endless journalistic vultures only too ready with pens and typewriters poised for the story of the record star who stopped selling records. A production agreement with another artist which eventually results in a record which receives lukewarm reviews can do no good even if it is largely, if not all, the fault of the artist. A venture into a stage play or a film for Barry must result in instant success. People will not judge him on the basis that what he is doing is his first play or film.

And the failure in one of these fields can adversely affect the others. A failed album can mean lack of interest from film people who might think his star is fading. A film which receives a battering from the critics and low attendances can lead to a lessening of interest in his record activities. There are countless other permutations!

Manilow's supporters in the media and his fans would insist there is no fear of the artist finding life difficult in the next few years. Certainly there is more in favour of this view than any other. Barry Manilow does look set for a happy recording time in the 1980s. There is no reason why he should not continue producing hit albums for other people. His proven skills on television and on stage suggest he could well translate successfully his various talents into film, if only someone would come up with the right part and the right script.

There is always, for any artist, another threat. It lies in the demands which are laid down by even the most well meaning. People can set their own standards which they think someone should reach. They do so with the best intentions in the world and often it has proved a millstone around someone's neck. In the case of Barry there are voices which forecast him as the next Sinatra, the male version of Barbra Streisand. He may well achieve this level of success but they increase unnecessary stress. At least Barry does have his feet firmly on the ground. Unlike some superstars of his status he does not surround himself with a vast entourage that cushions him from the real world. He is aware of what is happening at grass roots level. He is not shielded from the cold winds of reality. He takes an active interest in the business affairs which stem from his various musical talents. It was this aspect which caught the attention of the *Sunday Telegraph Colour*

Supplement's writer, Sue Read, when she visited Barry in Los Angeles.

Yet even here he is careful. Two weeks before he tours he ceases being involved in business activity. He told Sue Read that he does not dictate letters, take telephone calls or go to meetings during this period. His whole orientation is toward establishing the right mental balance. He told the journalist:

I have to demand more of myself in order to go on stage. Then I have to say to myself, 'Manilow, it's only a show, it's not life or death.' The fear I used to suffer was paralysing. I was scared. Before I go on stage I create a little scene in my head: I'm going out of my bedroom into my living room to show my friends a couple of songs. That way it works.

Barry does not smoke. He does not drink alcohol. He is not involved with drugs. He once said: 'I tried smoking joints (marijuana). I liked it for a month, three or four years ago, I had a very nice time getting pleasantly you know ... Frankly I didn't enjoy it.'

It helps Barry avoid some of the dangers which have faced and conquered innumerable pop stars, for the history of popular music is littered with the stories of promising and albeit highly successful people who fall victim to drugs and drink. Superstar status does make tough demands on the body. Numerous famous artists have told me of the stress and strain of continual recording and touring and the mental stress of staying ahead of whatever 'new' the music business throws up which can be a direct threat to their livelihood and general popularity.

Barry's lifestyle almost seems staid in comparison with the so-called glamorous habits of stars whose names regularly adorn the more racy pages of the press. He likes nothing better than, 'a good book, a good rhythm and blues record, conversation with friends having nothing whatsoever to do with the music industry'. He regards a real treat as simply engaging in what most people do – shopping.

It keeps him together as a person. It enables him to retain his position in the superstar bracket without undue mental stress.

Naturally this attitude doesn't gain him friends in some press circles. He is not good material for the gossip columns. Nor is he fodder for the next series on stars who came and went in a blaze of decadence. Yet he remains and some critics can only carp at his undoubted success and ever promising future. His fans appreciate these qualities of Barry. They like him as he is.

This is a view quite obviously held by the intimate circle of people around Barry. Stability is a rare thing in the music business. Obviously Barry gains the love and respect of manager Miles Lourie, his constant companion Linda Allen, and the gentleman with whom he has worked since Bell days – Ron Dante. Dante has been Barry's co-producer on countless tracks and in past times it was he who so enthused about Barry's talent that he persuaded famous TV and music business figure Don Kirshner to hear him at the Continental Baths.

Barry told me early summer 1981:

I never thought of performing. If you have a hit then your career can go places. I had one with 'Mandy' and Clive Davis was right. I just never thought about 'one day me' at the top.

My mother keeps saying to me, 'Get married, Barry, I want grandchildren.' I just keep on writing and performing. And I stay true to myself. Everything I've done and what I feel is truthful.

BARRY – IN HIS OWN WORDS

As quoted in magazines and newspapers over the years

'A lot of people in this business feel like suicide if a record fails or if an audience doesn't like them. But not me. I'd arrange songs for someone else or I'd write a jingle in a TV commercial. I'd play the piano in some bar.'

'I was very concerned about whether I was going to turn into Vic Damone or David Bowie. I respect them both, but I don't want their audiences. No, that's not right either. Well, people would say, "Where do you fit in? What do you do?" and I didn't have an answer. And it used to bother them, but I don't want to have a category. I don't want … I wanna be me.'

'I'm a good musician, I think. When I watch myself on TV, I think, "Gee, I really like this guy. He's having a wonderful time. He's not trying that hard." I think that's it. That's why people like me – it's the honesty they can relate to.'

'I think that I make intelligent music and that my audience is intelligent.'

'The person I admire most is Paul Simon in the way that he handles his career and his life. He's not flamboyant and his music is most important. I like that whole feeling about Paul.'

'Now, who gives a damn about categories. I choose to make this music and I would do it again. I'd go back in the studios and make "Could It Be Magic" and "Mandy" and "I Write The Songs" just the same way. I'm just a guy who's doing his job.'

'I hope to hell that people buy my performance because they truly believe what I'm singing about. More than anything else, that audience has got to relate to the emotions in my material. On stage, my public sees me go through a considerable amount of joy, anger and pain. I'm as honest as I possibly can be when I'm up there, and I just can't part with any more of myself. But that's what touring is all about.'

'I grew up wanting to be Nelson Riddle. I'm only a fair singer. I write nice songs, but I'm a great arranger. If it all fell apart tomorrow, I'd be able to make a living as an arranger.'

'Retirement? When I'm 50-something. I might lie on a raft on the Riviera. The people who last 20 or 30 years in this business don't do it by accident.'

'I'm from nowhere, Brooklyn, up from nothing. I've worked my ass off to get here and I'm gonna work my ass off to stay here. I can't sleep at night for the music going round in my head.'

'If it all ended tomorrow, I sure wouldn't be upset, because I've had such a great time.'

'People relate to the things I sing about. We're shared common life experiences.'

'Basically I'm an idealist and a romantic, and I want to give people pleasure.'

'When I got out of high school, even though I was voted top musician and was always at the piano and playing the accordion and singing with my friends, it never really dawned on me that I was gonna do it for real. Music was my playtime. You gotta go out, work, and have a family.'

'Glamour plays an incredible part in my act. I put some rhinestones on my chest because I don't want to look like everybody else in the audience. When I go to a concert and see a guitar player come out with jeans and a workshirt – well, that's not showbusiness to me. So I put a little doodads on my shirt and my hair is a little blonder than that of the guys in the audience, and it's fun. It's make-believe.'

'I don't believe in this astrology crap but I am a Gemini. Geminis are supposed to have this double thing – one day hot, one day cold – and it's very true about me. Look at my music, at my career. It's been a little of everything.'

'The biggest challenge for me is to keep my feet on the ground to keep my sanity and not let stardom overtake me. I refuse to let it change my life and my values.'

'I try to do a little bit for everyone. They told me I was crazy in the beginning – that I had to go for one audience or I'd end up with none. Luckily I didn't take any notice.'

'I haven't been in love for a long while. Who has the time? I read somewhere it's either heart or art. The hardest part is coming home to nobody.'

'Look, why isn't it enough that I am who I am, writing music I like for people who want to listen. I have no problems with drugs or booze or dozens of different girls. But I'm happy, damn it! I'm enjoying my life, my music. I'm GLAD I have no problems.'

'I come out of a restaurant after a relaxing dinner and somebody screams my name, pushes a camera in my face and blinds me with a flash. I know it all comes with the territory, and that I'm not supposed to be offended but I always think, "How rude!" '

'I'm lucky and I know it. But success and money have not made much difference to me. I have some gold records on my wall and live in a bigger house with more things. But none of that is really important. It's the music which is.'

'I like my life to be quiet. I don't particularly like being in the papers. I don't like the performing aspect of it, the personality part of it at all. I love producing records, writing songs and that's my favourite place of all – in the background.'

'I do guarantee that whatever I do will be of the high quality people expect of me. My stuff will always be creative and will always have my personality in it. I mean you could put Earth, Wind & Fire behind me and it'd still sound like Barry Manilow.'

'The fact that I'm sitting here doing an interview with *Soul* obviously has nothing to do with the colour of my skin. It's because my music affects all people. The same with Dionne who I believe is the consummate singer. As a producer, I could only offer her imput on orchestrations and arrangements. Vocally there was nothing I could contribute.'

'When I learn a song the sentiment does get through to me.'

'It annoys me when reviewers say I don't sing like Caruso. Well, I know that! That's not the point.'

'I'd be far more upset if I thought I was losing a friend than if I thought I was losing a record.'

'Look, I love my job, it's the best job I ever had. We all like to get patted on the back, and I love to get patted on the back by my audience.'

The fans and the critics on Barry – on stage and as a person

'Barry is the most gorgeous guy I've ever seen. To put it bluntly, he's got the lot plus a little bit extra!'

Faith Griffiths, fan.

'I've seen Manilow perform countless times over the last few years, and although I've never been a dyed-in-the-wool fan, I've never seen him give a bad performance. In the end, Barry Manilow is a talent I must respect.'

Mitchell Fink, Los Angeles *Herald Examiner*.

'Manilow the performer overshadows the excellent Manilow the songwriter. He is sheer personality and charisma on stage, and a fine talent.'

Frank Barron, *Hollywood Reporter*.

'There is one star who shines among them all. Barry

Manilow. His music sets a warm fire burning in the hearts of his fans.'

Linda Nash, fan, USA.

'Even on its own MOR level, Manilow's music lacks the sophistication and wit of Cole Porter and the best of the pre-rock writers. Measured against his peers, the music remains undistinguished.'

Robert Hilburn, *Los Angeles Times*.

'Just nice, what I expected him to be, what I hoped he'd be.'

Ann Silverman, fan, after a meeting with Barry.

'I've found my special guy and my very, very special friend, I've found – Barry.'

Lesley Karen Barwood, fan.

'The man is something of an entertainment miracle.'

Richard Christiansen, *Chicago News*.

'It was the end and the crowd filed out of the auditorium, chatting about the concert. Even those who evidently had to be "dragged along" to the event were heard to mildly comment, "Well … it was quite a show." '

Sue Leonard, *Times Press*, Streator, Illinois.

'As he is surrounded by groups of record company sycophants and junior executives, one cannot help but wonder about the qualities which have in fact taken him to the top.'

Simon Kinnersley, *Daily Mail*.

'For a man who must, by now, be convinced by the sheer

statistics of his success, there is an air of amazed modesty which hangs over him.'

Danae Brook, London *Evening News*.

'Though Barry Manilow approached the door to stardom at a careful-but-steady walk, he burst through it like Kojak nailing a dope pusher.'

Robert Wilson, *Press Scimitar*, Memphis.

'Manilow carries the hour with his music, his singing, his wit, his semi-dancing, but most of all with that too rare trait: charm.'

Variety on *The Second Barry Manilow TV Special*, 1978.

'And yet this ghastly creature had an undeniably excellent voice, had a repertoire that included an above-average share of songs that he has made minor contemporary standards.'

Robin Denselow, *The Guardian*.

'He doesn't remotely look like the inspiration for a million romantic fantasies. Not this skinny, hollow-cheeked singer with the golf ball Adam's apple who takes the stage with all the aplomb of a gawky schoolboy. But the transformation begins the second he raises his distinctive, half-throaty, half-nasal voice in song.'

Chip Orton, *US*, USA.

'But the British will love you for ever – if you let them.'

Bart Mills, *Daily Mail*.

'To call his act plastic would be an insult to ICI.'

Tune In.

'Possibly knocking on the Emmy door with his latest special, Manilow has proved why he's the reigning superstar of romantic-ballads with this entertaining program of hits.'

> Hanford Searl reviewing *The Third Barry Manilow Special*, ABC-TV, *Billboard*.

'Manilow's voice throughout is excellent, displaying a range and a clarity which is hard to beat.'

> David Lawrenson, *International Musician*.

'His music is at once grown-up (he's no teenage idol) and sexless. His fans don't fancy him the way their children or friends fancy David Essex or Billy Idol. Manilow is a symbol not of sex and possibility, but of affluence and achievement.'

> Simon Frith, *Melody Maker*.

'But in everything Manilow performs he has a tough, city grace about him – like Cagney hoofing it in the old flicks, or George Burns doing a monologue about yesterdays on the Lower East Side. Like them, he's also very proud of his profession and how well he's done in it. He has every reason to be.'

> Peter Reilly, *Stereo Review*.

'Part of Manilow's appeal is that he does more than perform. The man is his music. If the song is emotional, so is he.'

> Carol Wallace, *Philadelphia Daily News*.

' "He's just adorable."
 ' "I love him. He's so cute."
 ' "He's wonderful."
 'No, these aren't remarks overheard at the nearest hospital's nursery. They were overheard in the lobby at the Academy of Music.'

> Janet Melaragni, *News of Delaware County*.

'He has an exceptional ear for melody, whether he writes the songs or picks them from the works of others. It is difficult to think of another consistent contemporary hit-maker who has recorded so many memorable tunes.'

Robert Palmer, *New York Times*.

'At the top of his show, Barry Manilow — in his Riviera debut — promises to cram so much music into his timeslot, "you won't know what song to go out humming." He fulfils that promise and much more ...'

Mark Tan, Las Vegas Review, *Hollywood Reporter*.

'He's one entertainer who knows what the people who come paid to hear. And more important, how to deliver it.'

Gerry Baker, *Morning Star-Telegram*, Ft. Worth, Texas.

'He has an irresistible touch on plain old-fashioned pop songs, and it's easy to see how he has won the hearts of middle America.'

Ray Coleman, *Melody Maker*.

'But Manilow is the kind of guy who doesn't like to settle for anything less than No. 1. And he normally gets where he says is going.'

George Welsh, *Paisley Daily Express*.

'Onstage, though, you can call him anything you'd like, but one thing stands out that clearly defines his success: Barry Manilow is a slick, skilful entertainer who deftly pulls heartstrings to move his audience from one emotion to the next.'

Robert Stephen Spitz, *Crawdaddy*.

'As a musician and arranger, Manilow proves again that he is tops at his job.'

> Review of 'Even Now', Steven Gaines,
> *Circus* magazine, US.

'Barry and his music have changed my life. I've made friends and done things that I would have said were impossible.'

> Christine Richards, fan.

'I think we all love Barry in every way it is possible to love someone. As a friend, a son, a member of the family, the "boy next door" – and, of course, he has tremendous sex-appeal!'

> Sheila Reynolds, fan.

'He is every woman's sweetheart
  'Every mother's son
  'Every little girl's big brother
  'And every man's best chum.'

> Ursula Stunt, fan.

DISCOGRAPHY:

(for the UK and USA)

1. **Barry Manilow.** *(Bell 1129). Released autumn 1973.*
Produced by Barry Manilow and Ron Dante. Arranged and conducted by Barry Manilow.
Rhythm Section: Piano: Barry Manilow. Electric Guitar: Dick Frank. Acoustic guitar: Stuart Scharff. Bass: Stu Woods. Drums: Steve Gadd. Congas and tambourine: Norman Pride.

Side One:

1. 'Sing It'. 1:16. Barry and Grandpa Joe Manilow. Times Square, 1948.
2. 'Sweetwater Jones'. 2:29. Music and lyrics by Barry Manilow. Bass: Russell George. Congas: Bobby Matas. Percussion: Lee Gurst. Background vocals: Gail Kantor, Merle Miller, Melissa Manchester, Ron Dante. Recorded at Associated Sound Studios, NYC by Jerome Gasper.
Remixed at Asssociated Sound Studios, NYC by Artie Freedman.
3. 'Cloudburst'. 2:25 Music and lyrics by Leroy Kirkland, Jimmy Harris and Jon Hendriks. All vocals: Barry Manilow. Recorded and mixed at A & R Sound

Studios, NYC by Elliot Scheiner.

4. 'One Of These Days'. 2:54. Music and lyrics by Barry Manilow. Guitar solo: Stuart Scharff. Background vocals: Ron Dante and Barry Manilow.
Recorded and mixed at A & R Sound Studios, NYC by Elliot Scheiner.

5. 'Oh My Lady'. 3:26. Music and lyrics by Barry Manilow and Adrienne Anderson. Guitar solo: Dick Frank.
Recorded and mixed at A & R Studios, NYC by Elliot Scheiner.

6. 'I Am Your Child'. 2:14. Music by Barry Manilow. Lyrics by Marty Panzer. Bass: Russell George. Strings arranged by Barry Manilow.
Recorded at Associated Sound Studios, NYC by Jerome Gasper.

Side Two:

1. 'Could It Be Magic'. 7:11. Inspired by Prelude in C Minor – F. Chopin. Music and lyrics by Barry Manilow and Adrienne Anderson.
Background vocals: Gail Kantor, Merle Miller, Laurel Masse, Ron Dante, Pamela Pentony, Robert Danz, Adrienne Anderson, Kathe Green, Jane Schekter, Jane Stuart, Sheilah Rae.
Recorded and mixed at A & R Studios, NYC by Elliot Scheiner.

2. 'Seven More Years'. 3:35. Music by Barry Manilow. Lyrics by Barry Manilow and Marty Panzer.
Recorded and mixed at A & R Sound Studios, NYC by Elliot Scheiner.

3. 'Flashy Lady'. 3:57. Music and lyrics by Ron Dante and Marty Panzer. Guitar: Bon Mann, Ron Dante. Bass: Bob Babbit. Drums: Andrew Smith. Percussion: Jim Maeulen.
Recorded and Mixed at A & R Sound Studios, NYC by Elliot Scheiner.

4. 'Friends'. 3:05. Music and lyrics by Buzzy Linhart and Mark Klingman. Background voices: Gail Kantor, Merle Miller, Laurel Masse.
Recorded and mixed at A & R Sound Studios, NYC by Elliot Scheiner.
5. 'Sweet Life (Mama Can Ya Hear Me)'. 3:14. Music and lyrics by Barry Manilow. Bass: Russell George. Background voices: Gail Kantor, Merle Miller, Melissa Manchester.
Recorded at Associated Sound Studios, NYC by Jerome Gasper.

Album playing time: Side One: 14.44. Side Two: 21.20.
Total time: 36.04.

2. **Barry Manilow I**. (*Arista AL 4007*). Released June 1975 (re-released version of **Barry Manilow**. Bell 1129).

3. **Barry Manilow II** (*Arista ARTY 100*). *Released autumn 1974*.
Produced by Barry Manilow and Ron Dante.
Rhythm arrangements by Barry Manilow. Background voices: Ron Dante and Barry Manilow.
Recorded at the Hit Factory, NYC and Media Sound Studios, NYC. Engineers: Bruce Tergesen, Harry Maslin and Michael Delugg.

Side One:

1. 'I Want To Be Somebody's Baby'. 4:18. Music by Barry Manilow. Lyrics by Enoch Anderson.
2. 'Early Morning Strangers'. 3:24. Music by Barry Manilow. Lyrics by Hal David.
3. 'Mandy'. 3:32. Music and lyrics by Richard Kerr and Scott English.
4. 'The Two Of Us'. 3:05. Music by Barry Manilow. Lyrics by Marty Panzer.

5. 'Something's Comin' Up'. 2:51. Music and lyrics by Barry Manilow.

Side Two:

1. 'It's A Miracle'. 3:58. Music by Barry Manilow. Lyrics by Barry Manilow and Marty Panzer.
2. 'Avenue C'. 2:37. Music by Buck Clayton. Lyrics by Jon Hendriks and Dave Lambert.
3. 'My Baby Loves Me'. Music and lyrics by Sylvia Moy, William Stevenson and Ivy Hunter.
4. 'Sandra'. 4:35. Music by Barry Manilow. Lyrics by Enoch Anderson.
5. 'Home Again'. 5:34. Music by Barry Manilow. Lyrics by Marty Panzer.

Album playing time. Side One: 17.10. Side Two: 20.02. Total time: 37.12.

4. **Tryin' To Get The Feeling** (*Arista ARTY 123*). *Released October 1975.*
Produced by Barry Manilow and Ron Dante.
Rhythm tracks arranged by Barry Manilow.
Barry's band: Piano: Barry Manilow, Guitar: Sid McGinnis. Drums and Percussion: Lee Gurst. Keyboards: Alan Axelrod. Bass: Steve Donaghey. Studio musicians: Guitar: Charlie Brown. Congas, Bongas, Shaker: Jimmy Maeulen. Background vocals: The Flashy Ladies: Debra Byrd, Ramona Brooks and Reparata (Lorraine Mazzola), Ron Dante and Barry Manilow.
Recorded at Media Sound Studios, NYC. Engineer: Michael Delugg.

Side One:

1. 'New York City Rhythm'. Music by Barry Manilow. Lyrics by Marty Panzer.
2. 'Tryin' To Get The Feeling Again'. Music and lyrics by David Pomeranz.

3. 'Why Don't We Live Together' Music and lyrics by Phil Galdston and Peter Thom.
4. 'Bandstand Boogie'. Music by G. Albertine, L. Elgart, Bob Horn and L. Elgart. Special lyrics by Bruce Sussman and Barry Manilow. All vocals – 32 voices – Barry Manilow. Horns arranged by Arif Mardin.
5. 'You're Leavin' Too Soon'. Music by Barry Manilow. Lyrics by Enoch Anderson. Pedal Steel Guitar: Sid McGinnis.
6. 'She's A Star'. Music by Barry Manilow. Lyrics by Enoch Anderson. Strings and horns arranged by Arif Mardin.

Side Two:

1. 'I Write The Songs'. Music and lyrics by Bruce Johnston. Strings and horns arranged by Gerald Alters.
2. 'As Sure As I'm Standin' Here'. Music by Barry Manilow. Lyrics by Adrienne Anderson. Strings arranged by Norman Harris and recorded at Sigma Sound Studios, Philadelphia.
3. 'A Nice Boy Like Me'. Music by Barry Manilow. Lyrics by Enoch Anderson. Strings and horns arranged by Norman Harris and recorded at Sigma Studios, Philadelphia.
4. 'Lay Me Down'. Music and lyrics by Larry Weiss. Strings arranged by Joe Renzetti.
5. 'Beautiful Music'. Music by Barry Manilow. Lyrics by Marty Panzer.

5. **This One's For You** (*Arista ARTY 137*). *Released July 1976.* Produced by Ron Dante and Barry Manilow. Arranged by Barry Manilow.
Background vocals: Lady Flash: Monica Burruss, Debra Byrd, Reparata, Barry Manilow and Ron Dante.
Recorded and mixed at Media Sound, NYC. Engineer: Michael Delugg.

Side One:

1. 'This One's For You'. Music by Barry Manilow. Lyrics by Marty Panzer.
2. 'Daybreak'. Music by Barry Manilow. Lyrics by Adrienne Anderson. Strings and horns orchestrated by Charlie Calello. Drums: Ron Zito. Bass: Will Lee. Guitars: David Spinoza and Gerry Friedman. Piano: Barry Manilow. Congas: Carlos Martin.
3. 'You Oughta Be Home With Me'. Music by Barry Manilow. Lyrics by Adrienne Anderson. Strings and horns orchestrated by Van Mccoy. Drums: Ron Zito. Guitars: David Spinoza and Gerry Friedman. Keyboards: Paul Schaeffer. Congas: Carlos Martin.
4. 'Jump Shout Boogie'. Music by Barry Manilow. Lyrics by Barry Manilow and Bruce Sussman. Horns orchestrated by Dick Berkhe. Drums: Ron Zito. Guitars: David Spinoza and Gerry Friedman. Keyboards: Paul Schaeffer. Congas and Grunts: Carlos Martin.
5. 'Weekend In New England'. Music and lyrics by Randy Edelman. Strings and horns orchestrated by Gerald Altere. Drums: Lee Gurst. Guitar: Richard Resnicoff. Piano: Barry Manilow.

Side Two:

1. 'Riders To The Stars'. Music by Barry Manilow. Lyrics by Adrienne Anderson. Strings and horns orchestrated by Gerald Alters and Barry Manilow. Drums: Ron Zito. Bass: Will Lee. Guitar: David Spinoza and Gerry Friedman. Keyboards: Paul Schaeffer. Piano: Barry Manilow. Congas: Carlos Martin.
2. 'Let Me Go'. Music by Barry Manilow. Lyrics by Marty Panzer. Horns orchestrated by Dick Berkhe. Drums: Ron Zito. Bass: Will Lee. Guitars: David Spinoza and Richard Resnicoff. Keyboards: Paul Schaeffer. Piano:

Barry Manilow. Congas: Carlos Martin.

3. 'Looks Like We Made It'. Music by Richard Kerr. Lyric by Will Jennings. Strings and horns orchestrated by Gerald Alters. Drums: Lee Gurst. Bass: Steve Donaghey. Guitar: Richard Resnicoff. Keyboards: Alan Axelrod. Piano: Barry Manilow.

4. 'Say The Words'. Music and lyrics by Barry Manilow. Drums: Lee Gurst. Bass: Steve Donaghey. Guitar: Richard Resnicoff. Dennis Farac and Ron Dante. Keyboards: Alan Axelrod.

5. 'All The Time'. Music by Barry Manilow. Lyrics by Marty Panzer and Barry Manilow. Strings and horns orchestrated by Gerald Alters. Drums: Lee Gurst. Guitars: Richard Resnicoff and Dennis Farac. Bass: Steve Donaghey. Keyboards: Alan Axelrod. Piano: Barry Manilow.

6. 'Why Don't We See The Show Again' Music by Barry Manilow. Lyrics by Adrienne Anderson. Strings and horns orchestrated by Gerald Alters. Drums: Ron Zito. Bass: Will Lee. Guitars: Richard Resnicoff and David Spinoza. Keyboards: Paul Schaeffer. Piano: Barry Manilow.

6. **Barry Manilow Live** *(Arista DARTY 3). Released May 1977.* Orchestrations by Gerald Alters. Additional orchestrations by Barry Manilow, Norman Harris, Dick Berkhe, Arif Mardin, Charlie Calello and Joe Renzetti. The City Rhythm Band: Drums: Lee Gurst, Bass: Steve Donaghey, Keyboards: Alan Axelrod, Congas: Harold 'Ricardo' Alexander, Guitar: Keith Loving, Piano: Barry Manilow. Orchestra conducted by Lee Gurst. Background vocals: Lady Flash: Debra Byrd, Reparata and Monica Burruss. Additional guitar: Sid McGinnis.
Recorded at the Uric Theatre, New York City. Live recording engineer: John Venable. Mixed at Media Sound Studios, New York City. Engineer: Michael Delugg.

Side One:

1. 'Riders To The Stars'. Music by Barry Manilow. Lyrics by Adrienne Anderson.
2. 'Why Don't We Live Together' Music and lyrics by Phil Galdston and Peter Thom.
3. 'Looks Like We Made It'. Music by Richard Kerr. Lyrics by Will Jennings.
4. 'New York City Rhythm'. Music by Barry Manilow. Lyrics by Marty Panzer.

Side Two:

1. 'A Very Strange Medley (VSM)'. Recorded at Ravina Festival, Chicago.
(a) 'Grab A Bucket Of Chicken' (Kentucky Fried Chicken).
(b) 'State Farm Insurance' (Like A Good Neighbour). Music and lyrics by Barry Manilow, Jerry Gavin and Keith Reinhard.
(c) 'Stridex'. Music and lyrics by Barry Manilow.
(d) 'Stuck On Me' (Band-Aid). Music and lyrics by Barry Manilow and Donald B. Wood.
(e) 'Bathroom Bowl Blues' (Green Bowlene). Music and lyrics by Barry Manilow and Lois Wise.
(f) 'The Most Original Soft Drink Ever' (Dr Pepper). Music and lyrics by Randy Newman and Jake Holmes.
(g) 'Feelin' Free' (Pepsi Cola). Music and lyrics by Ellen Starr and Joe McNeil.
(h) 'McDonalds (You Deserve A Break Today)'. Music and lyrics by Keith Reinhard, Richard Hazlett, Ed Farran, Sid Woloshin and Kevin Gavin.
2. 'Jump Shout Boogie Medley'.
(a) 'Jump Shout Boogie'. Music by Barry Manilow. Lyrics by Barry Manilow and Bruce Sussman.
(b) 'Avenue C'. Music and lyrics by Jon Hendriks. Dave Lambert and Buck Clayton.

(c) 'Jumpin' At The Woodside'. Music and lyrics by Jon Hendriks and Count Basie.

(d) 'Cloudburst'. Music and lyrics by Jimmie Harris, Jon Hendriks and Leroy Kirkland.

(e) 'Bandstand Boogie'. Music by C. Albertine, Bob Horn, Les Elgart, Larry Elgart. Special lyrics by Barry Manilow and Bruce Sussman.

3. 'This One's For You'. Music by Barry Manilow. Lyrics by Marty Panzer.

Side Three:

1. 'Beautiful Music' (Part I). Music by Barry Manilow. Lyrics by Marty Panzer.
2. 'Daybreak'. Music by Barry Manilow. Words by Adrienne Anderson.
3. 'Lay Me Down'. Music and lyrics by Larry Weiss.
4. 'Weekend In New England'. Music and lyrics by Randy Edelman.
5. 'Studio Musician'. Music and lyrics by Rupert Holmes.

Side Four:

1. 'Beautiful Music' (Part II). Music by Barry Manilow. Lyrics by Marty Panzer.
2. 'Could It Be Magic'/'Mandy'. Music by Barry Manilow and lyrics by Adrienne Anderson/Music and lyrics by Richard Kerr and Scott English.
3. 'It's A Miracle'. Music by Barry Manilow. Lyrics by Barry Manilow and Marty Panzer.
4. 'It's Just Another New Year's Eve'. Music by Barry Manilow. Lyrics by Marty Panzer.
5. 'I Write The Songs'. Music and lyrics by Bruce Johnston.
6. 'Beautiful Music' (Part III). Music by Barry Manilow. Lyrics by Marty Panzer.

7. **Barry Manilow – Greatest Hits** (*Arista AZL 8601*). *Released 1978*.
Produced by Barry Manilow and Ron Dante. Engineer: Michael Delugg.

Side One:

1. 'Mandy'. 3:15. Music and lyrics by Richard Kerr and Scott English.
   Taken from Barry Manilow II.
2. 'New York City Rhythm'. 4:42. Music by Barry Manilow. Lyrics by Marty Panzer.
   Taken from Tryin' To Get The Feeling.
3. 'Ready To Take A Chance Again'. 3:01. (From the film Foul Play.) Music by Charles Fox. Lyrics by Norman Gimbel.
4. 'Looks Like We Made It'. 3:33. Music by Richard Kerr. Lyrics by Will Jennings.
   Taken from the album This One's For You.
5. 'Daybreak'. 3:36. Music by Barry Manilow. Lyrics by Adrienne Anderson.
   Taken from This One's For You.

Side Two:

1. 'Can't Smile Without You'. 3:13. Music and lyrics by Chris Arnold, Dave Martin and Geoff Murrow.
   Taken from the album Even Now.
2. 'It's A Miracle'. 3:42. Music by Barry Manilow. Lyrics by Barry Manilow and Marty Panzer.
   Album: Barry Manilow II.
3. 'Even Now'. 3:28. Music by Barry Manilow. Lyrics by Marty Panzer.
   Taken from the album Even Now.
4. 'Bandstand Boogie'. 2:49. Music by C. Albertine, L. Elgart, Bob Horn and L. Elgart. Special lyrics by Bruce Sussman and Barry Manilow.
   Taken from the album Tryin' To Get The Feeling.

Side Three:

1. 'Could It Be Magic'. 6:50. Inspired by Prelude in C Minor – F. Chopin. Music and lyrics by Barry Manilow and Adrienne Anderson.
   Taken from album Barry Manilow I.
2. 'Somewhere In The Night'. 3:26. Music by Richard Kerr. Lyrics by Will Jennings.
   Taken from album Even Now.
3. 'Jump Shout Boogie'. 3:03. Music by Barry Manilow. Lyrics by Barry Manilow and Bruce Sussman.
   Taken from album This One's For You.
4. 'Weekend In New England'. 3:43. Music and lyrics by Randy Edelman.
   Taken from album This One's For You.

Side Four:

1. 'This One's For You'. 3:25. Music by Barry Manilow. Lyrics by Marty Panzer.
   Taken from album This One's For You.
2. 'Copacabana' (Disco). 5:46. Music by Barry Manilow. Lyrics by Bruce Sussman and Jack Feldman.
   Taken from album Even Now.
3. 'Beautiful Music.' 4:32. Music by Barry Manilow. Lyrics by Marty Panzer.
   Taken from album Tryin' To Get The Feeling.
4. 'I Write The Songs'. 3:51. Music and lyrics by Bruce Johnston.
   Taken from album Tryin' To Get The Feeling.

8. **Manilow Magic** (*The Best of Barry Manilow*) (*Arista ARTV 2*). *Released February 1979.*
Produced by Barry Manilow and Ron Dante. Engineer: Michael Delugg.

Side One:

1. 'Mandy'. 3:21. Music and lyrics by Richard Kerr and Scott English.
   Album: Barry Manilow II.
2. 'New York City Rhythm'. 4:42. Music by Barry Manilow. Lyrics by Marty Panzer.
   Album: Tryin' To Get The Feeling.
3. 'Looks Like We Made It'. 3:33. Music by Richard Kerr. Lyrics by Will Jennings.
   Album: This One's For You.
4. 'Can't Smile Without You'. 3:12. Music and lyrics by Chris Arnold, David Martin and Geoff Morrow.
   Album: Even Now.
5. 'Ready To Take A Chance Again'. 3:01. (From the film Foul Play.) Music by Charles Fox. Lyrics by Norman Gimbel.
   Album: Barry Manilow – Greatest Hits.
6. 'Tryin' To Get The Feeling Again'. 3:50. Music and lyrics by David Pomeranz.
   Album: Tryin' To Get The Feeling.

Side Two:

1. 'Could It Be Magic'. 6:48. Inspired by Prelude in C Minor – F. Chopin. Music and lyrics by Barry Manilow and Adrienne Anderson.
   Album: Barry Manilow I.
2. 'Copacabana'. 5:44. Music by Barry Manilow. Lyrics by Bruce Sussman and Jack Feldman.
   Album: Even Now.
3. 'Weekend In New England'. 3:43. Music and lyrics by Randy Edelman.
   Album: This One's For You.
4. 'It's A Miracle'. 3:43. Music by Barry Manilow. Lyrics by Barry Manilow and Marty Panzer.
   Album: Barry Manilow II.

5. 'All The Time'. 3:14. Music by Barry Manilow. Lyrics by Marty Panzer and Barry Manilow.
   Album: This One's For You.
6. 'I Write The Songs'. 3:54. Music and lyrics by Bruce Johnston.
   Album: Tryin' To Get The Feeling.

9. **Even Now** (*Arista SPART 1047*). *Released April 1978.*
Produced by Ron Dante and Barry Manilow.
Rhythm section: Drums: Ronnie Zito. Piano: Barry Manilow. Guitar: Mitch Holder. Bass: Will Lee. Keyboards: Bill Mays. Percussion: Allan Estes.
Background voices: Ron Dante and Barry Manilow.
Recorded at A & M Studios, Hollywood, California, July through November 1977. engineer: Michael Delugg. Assistant Engineer: Derek Dunan.

Side One:

1. 'Copacabana (At The Copa)'. 4:08. Music by Barry Manilow. Lyrics by Bruce Sussman and Jack Feldman. Orchestration by Artie Butler. Background voices: Ginger Blake, Linda Dillard and Laura Creamer.
2. 'Somewhere In The Night'. 3:26. Music by Richard Kerr. Lyrics by Will Jennings. Orchestration by Dick Berkhe. Bass: Bob Babbit. Guitar: Jeff Mirinov. Percussion: Jimmy Maelen. Drums: Jimmy Young. Electric piano: Paul Shaeffer. Piano: Barry Manilow. Recorded at the Media Sound Studios, New York City.
3. 'A Linda Song'. 3:20. Music by Barry Manilow. Lyrics by Enoch Anderson. Orchestration by Richard Winzeler. Guitar: Lee Ritenour.
4. 'Can't Smile Without You'. 3:13. Music and lyrics by Chris Arnold, David Martin and Geoff Morrow. Orchestration by Artie Butler.
5. 'Leavin' In The Morning'. 3:25. Music by Barry

Manilow. Lyrics by Marty Panzer. Strings arranged by Barry Manilow.
6. 'Where Do I Go From Here'. 3:07. Music and lyrics by Parker McGee. Orchestration by Jimmie Haskell.

Side Two:

1. 'Even Now'. 3:28. Music by Barry Manilow. Lyrics by Marty Panzer. Orchestration by Artie Butler.
2. 'I Was A Fool (To Let You Go)'. 3:29. Music by Barry Manilow. Lyrics by Marty Panzer. Orchestration by Artie Butler.
3. 'Losing Touch'. 2:40. Music by Barry Manilow. Lyrics by Bruce Sussman and Jack Feldman. Orchestration by Gordon Haskell.
4. 'I Just Want To Be The One In Your Life'. 3:39. Music and lyrics by Michael Price and Dan Walsh. Orchestration by Jimmie Haskell.
5. 'Starting Again'. 2:40. Music by Barry Manilow. Lyrics by Marty Panzer.
6. 'Sunrise'. 3:16. Music and lyrics by Barry Manilow and Adrienne Anderson. Orchestration by Jimmie Haskell. Guitar: Jay Graydon.

10. **One Voice** (*Arista SPART 1106*). *Released September 1979.* Produced by Ron Dante and Barry Manilow.
Rhythm tracks arranged by Barry Manilow. Orchestration by Artie Butler, Rhythm Section: Piano: Barry Manilow. Drums: Ed Greene. Guitar: Mitch Holder. Synthesizer: Michael Boddicker. Keyboards: Bill Mays. Bass: Will Lee. Percussion: Alan Estes.
Recorded at United Western Studios and Allen Zentz Recording, Hollywood. Engineer: Michael Delugg.

Side One:

1. 'One Voice'. 3:01. 40 Background voices sung by Barry Manilow.

2. '(Why Don't We Try) A Slow Dance'. 4:16. Music by Barry Manilow. Lyrics by Bruce Sussman and Jack Feldman. Strings and horns orchestrated by Jimmie Haskell. Drums: Jim Gordon. Keyboards: Jai Winding. Bass: David Hungate. Background vocals: Ron Dante and Barry Manilow.

3. 'Rain'. 4:48. Music by Barry Manilow. Lyrics by Adrienne Anderson. Background vocals sung by Ron Dante, Barry Manilow, Monica Burruss, Reparata and Muffy Hendricks.

4. 'Ships'. 4:06. Music and lyrics by Ian Hunter. Bass: Dennis Belfield. Synthesizer: Ian Underwood. Background vocals sung by Ron Dante and Barry Manilow.

5. 'You Could Show Me'. 1:45. Music by Barry Manilow. Lyrics by Bruce Sussman and Jack Feldman.

6. 'I Don't Want To Walk Without You'. 3:54. Music by Julie Styne. Lyrics by Frank Loesser. Background vocals sung by Ron Dante and Barry Manilow.

Side Two:

1. 'Who's Been Sleeping In My Bed'. 4:36. Music by Barry Manilow. Lyrics by Marty Panzer. Synthesizer: Michael Boddiker/Ian Underwood. Background vocals sung by Ron Dante, Barry Manilow, Monica Burruss, Reparata and Muffy Hendricks.

2. 'Where Are They Now' 3:59. Background vocals sung by Ron Dante and Barry Manilow.

3. 'Bobbie Lee (What's The Difference, I Gotta Live)'. 3:32. Music by Barry Manilow. Lyrics by Enoch Anderson. Sax solo: Jim Horn. Background vocals by Ron Dante and Barry Manilow.

4. 'When I Wanted You'. 3:31. Music and lyrics by Gino Cunico. Background vocals sung by Ron Dante and Barry Manilow.

5. 'Sunday Father'. 2:51. Music by Barry Manilow. Lyrics by Enoch Anderson.

11. **Barry** (*Arista DART 2*). *Released November 1980*

Side One:

1. 'Lonely Together'. 4:19. Music and lyrics by Kenny Nolan. Produced by Barry Manilow. Rhythm track arranged by Barry Manilow and Artie Butler. Strings and horns arranged by Artie Butler. Piano: Barry Manilow. Drums: Carlos Vega. Fender Rhodes: David Wheatley. Guitar: Dennis Belfield. Pedal steel guitar: JayDee Maness. Calliope: Artie Butler. Background vocals: Kevin DiSimone, James Jolis, Jimmy Haas and Jon Joyce.

2. 'Bermuda Triangle'. Music by Barry Manilow. Lyrics by Bruce Sussman and Jack Feldman. Produced by Barry Manilow and Ron Dante. Rhythm track arranged by Barry Manilow. Strings and horns arranged by Artie Butler. Piano: Barry Manilow. Bass: Will Lee. Drums: Ron Zito. Guitar: Jeff Mironov, Dean Parks. Percussion: Jimmy Maelen, Alan Estes. Keyboards: Paul Schaeffer. Steel drum: Robert Greenidge. Background vocals: Barry Manilow, Ron Dante, Stephanie Spruill and Maxine Waters.
Recorded at Media Sound, New York City. Engineer: Michael Delugg. Strings and horns recorded and mixed at Evergreen Recording Studios, Burbank, California. Engineer: Murray McFadden.

3. 'I Made It Through The Rain'. 4:21. Music by Gerard Kenny. Lyrics by Drey Shepperd, Bruce Sussman, Jack Feldman and Barry Manilow. Produced by Barry Manilow and Ron Dante.
Rhythm track arranged by Barry Manilow and Victor Vanacore. Strings and horns arranged by Victor Vanacore. Piano: Barry Manilow. Guitar: John Pondel. Bass: Lou Shoch. Drums: Bud Harner. Synthesizer: Robert Marullo. Percussion: Ken Park. Fender Rhodes: Robert Marullo. Background vocals:

Kevin DiSimone, James Jolis, Pat Henderson, Robin Green, Jimmy Haas and Jon Joyce.
Recorded at Evergreen Recording Studios, Burbank, California. Mixed at Criteria Recording Studios, Miami, Florida. Engineer: Murray McFadden.

4. 'Twenty Four Hours A Day'. Music by Barry Manilow. Lyrics by Marty Panzer. Arranged by Barry Manilow. Piano: Barry Manilow. Bass: Lou Shoch. Synthesizer: Robert Marullo. Keyboards: Victor Vanacore. Guitar: John Pondel. Drums: Bud Harner. Percussion: Ken Park. Background vocals: Kevin DiSimone, James Jolis, Jimmy Haas and Jon Joyce.
Recorded and mixed at Evergreen Recording Studios, Burbank, California. Engineer: Murray McFadden. Assisted by Gary Luchs.

5. 'Dance Away'. 3:56. Music and lyrics by Troy Seals and Richard Kerr. Produced by Barry Manilow. Arranged by Barry Manilow. Piano: Barry Manilow. Bass: Dennis Belfield. Keyboards: Bill Mays. Percussion: Alan Estes. Guitar: Mitch Holder, Thom Rotella. Drums: Ed Greene. Synthesizer: Robert Marullo. Background vocals: Kevin DiSimone, James Jolis, Jimmy Haas and Jon Joyce.
Recorded and mixed at Evergreen Recording Studios, Burbank, California. Engineer: Murray McFadden. Assisted by Gary Luchs.

Side Two:

1. 'Life Will Go On'. 3:50. Music by Richard Kerr. Lyrics by John Bettis. Produced by Barry Manilow and Ron Dante. Rhythm track arranged by Barry Manilow and Artie Butler. Strings and horns arranged by Artie Butler. Piano: Barry Manilow. Drums: Bud Harner. Keyboards: Barry Manilow, Victor Vanacore. Guitar: John Pondel. Percussionist: Alan Estes. Keyboards: Barry Manilow, Victor Vanacore. Fender Rhodes:

Artie Butler. Background vocals: Jimmy Haas, Jon Joyce and Loren Farber.

Recorded and mixed at Evergreen Recording Studios, Burbank, California. Engineer: Murray McFadden. Assisted by Gary Luchs.

2. 'Only In Chicago'. 3:33. Music by Barry Manilow and Maurice White. Lyrics by Barry Manilow. Produced by Barry Manilow and Ron Dante. Arranged by Barry Manilow. Piano: Barry Manilow, Bass: Will Lee. Fender Rhodes: Tack Piano: Paul Schaeffer. Percussion: Jimmy Maelen. Drums: Ron Zito. Guitar: Jeff Mironov. Background vocals: Barry Manilow and Ron Dante. Rhythm tracks recorded at Media Sound, New York City.

Recorded and mixed at A & M Studios, Hollywood, California. Engineer: Michael Delugg.

3. 'The Last Duet'. 3:59. (Sung with Lily Tomlin.) Music by Barry Manilow. Lyrics by Bruce Sussman and Jack Feldman. Produced by Barry Manilow and Ron Dante. Rhythm Track arranged by Barry Manilow. Strings and horns arranged by Artie Butler. Piano: Barry Manilow. Guitar: Michael Landau. Drums: Ron Krasinski. Keyboard: Jerry Corbetta. Background vocals: Barry Manilow and Jimmy Haas. Rhythm tracks recorded at Dirk Dalton Recorders, Santa Monica, California. Engineer: Dirk Dalton.

Recorded and mixed at A & M Studios, Hollywood, California. Engineer: Michael Delugg.

4. 'London'. 5:18. Music by Barry Manilow. Lyrics by Bruce Sussman and Jack Feldman. Produced by Barry Manilow and Ron Dante. Arranged by Barry Manilow. Piano: Barry Manilow. Bass: Will Lee. Percussion: Jimmy Maelen. Synthesizer: Michael Boddicker. Drums: Ron Zito, Guitar: Jeff Mironov. Horns: Chuck Findlay. Rhythm Tracks recorded at Media Sound, New York City.

Recorded and mixed at Wally Heider Recording, Hollywood, California. Engineer: Michael Delugg.

5. 'We Still Have Time'. 4:12. (Theme tune from the motion picture *Tribute*.)

Music by Barry Manilow. Lyrics by Bruce Sussman and Jack Feldman. Produced by Barry Manilow and Ron Dante. Rhythm track arranged by Barry Manilow and Artie Butler. Strings and horns arranged by Barry Manilow and Artie Butler. Piano: Barry Manilow. Bass: Abraham Laboriel. Percussion: Alan Estes. Guitar: Dean Parks. Fred Tackett. Drums: Ed Greene. Harmonica: Tommy Morgan. Background vocals: Kevin DiSimone, James Jolis, Jimmy Haas and Jon Joyce.

Recorded and mixed at Evergreen Recording Studios, Burbank, California. Engineer: Murray McFadden. Assisted by Gary Luchs.

12. **If I Should Love Again** (*BM AN 1*). *Released September 1981.*

Side One:

1. 'The Old Songs' by David Pomeranz.
2. 'Let's Hang On' by B. Crewe, D. Randell and F. Linzer.
3. 'If I Should Love Again' by Barry Manilow.
4. 'Don't Fall in Love With Me' by John Bettis and Barry Manilow.
5. 'Break Down The Door' by Barry Manilow, Bob Gaudio and Enoch Anderson.

Side Two:

1. 'Somewhere Down The Road' by John Snow and Cynthia Weil.
2. 'No Other Love' by Barry Manilow and Adrienne Anderson.
3. 'Fools Get Lucky' by Barry Manilow and John Bettis.

4. 'I Often Changed The Room' by Barry Manilow.
5. 'Let's Take All Night To Say Goodbye' by Barry Manilow and John Bettis.
   Produced by Barry Manilow. Engineer: Michael Delugg.

AN A TO Z OF BARRY
MANILOW'S RECORDED SONGS

(With album source in brackets. Songs on If I Should Love
Again are not included.)

A

'A Linda Song' (Even Now. SPART 1047)

'A Nice Boy Like Me' (Tryin' To Get The Feeling. ARTY
123)

'A Slow Dance' (Why Don't We Try), (One Voice. SPART
1106)

'A Very Strange Medley' (Barry Manilow Live. DARTY 3)

'All The Time' (This One's For You. ARTY 137: Manilow
Magic ARTV 2)

'As Sure As I'm Standin' There' (Trying To Get The
Feeling. ARTY 123)

'Avenue C' (Barry Manilow II. ARTY 100)

B

'Bandstand Boogie' (Trying To Get The Feeling. ARTY
123: Greatest Hits. AZL 8601)

'Beautiful Music' (Trying To Get The Feeling. ARTY 123:
Barry Manilow Live. DARTY 3: Greatest Hits. AZL
8601)

'Beautiful Music II'. (Barry Manilow Live. DARTY 3)

'Beautiful Music III'. (Barry Manilow Live. DARTY 3)

'Bermuda Triangle' (Barry. DART 2)
'Bobbie Lee' (One Voice. SPART 1047)

C

'Can't Smile Without You' (Greatest Hits. AZL 8061:
    Manilow Magic. ARTV 2: Even Now. SPART 1047)
'Cloudburst' (Barry Manilow. Bell 1129)
'Copacabana (At The Copa)' (Even Now. SPART 1047)
'Copacabana (Disco)' (Greatest Hits. AZL 8061: Manilow
    Magic. ARTV 2)
'Could It Be Magic' (Barry Manilow. Bell 1129: Barry
    Manilow Live. DARTY 3: Greatest Hits. AZL 8061)

D

'Dance Away' (Barry. DART 2)
'Daybreak' (This One's For You. ARTY 137: Barry
    Manilow Live. DARTY 3: Greatest Hits. AZL 8601)

E

'Early Morning Strangers' (Barry Manilow II. ARTY 100)
'Even Now' (Greatest Hits. AZL 8601: Even Now. SPART
    1047)

F

'Flashy Lady' (Barry Manilow. Bell 1129)
'Friends' (Barry Manilow. Bell 1129)

H

'Home Again' (Barry Manilow II. ARTY 100)

I

'I Am Your Child' (Barry Manilow. Bell 1129)
'I Don't Want To Walk Without You' (One Voice. SPART
    1106)
'I Just Want To Be The One In Your Life' (Even Now.
    SPART 1047)

'I Made It Through The Rain' (Barry. DART 2)

'I Want To Be Somebody's Baby' (Barry Manilow II. ARTY 100)

'I Was A Fool' (Even Now. SPART 1047)

'I Write The Songs' (Tryin' to Get The Feeling. ARTY 123: Barry Manilow Live. DARTY 3: Greatest Hits. AZL 8601: Manilow Magic. ARTV 2)

'It's A Miracle' (Barry Manilow II. ARTY 100: Barry Manilow Live. DARTY 3: Greatest Hits. AZL 8601: Manilow Magic. ARTV 2)

'It's Just Another New Year's Eve' (Barry Manilow Live. DARTY 3)

L

'Lay Me Down' (Tryin' To Get The Feeling. ARTV 123)

'Let Me Go' (This One's For You. ARTY 137)

'Life Will Go On' (Barry. DART 2)

'London' (Barry. DART 2)

'Lonely Together' (Barry. DART 2)

'Looks Like We Made It' (This One's For You. ARTY 137: Barry Manilow Live. DARTY 3: Greatest Hits. AZL 8601: Manilow Magic. ARTV 2)

'Losing Touch' (Even Now. SPART 1047)

M

'Mandy' (Barry Manilow II. ARTY 100: Greatest Hits. AZL 8061: Manilow Magic. ARTV 2).

'My Baby Loves Me' (Barry Manilow II. ARTY 100)

N

'New York City Rhythm' (Tryin' To Get The Feeling. ARTY 123: Barry Manilow Live. ARTY 3: Greatest Hits. AZL 8601: Manilow Magic. ARTV 2)

O

'Oh My Lady' (Barry Manilow. Bell 1129)

'One Of Those Days' (Barry Manilow. Bell 1129)
'One Voice' (One Voice. SPART 1106)
'Only In Chicago' (Barry. DART 2)

R
'Rain' (One Voice. SPART 1106)
'Ready To Take A Chance Again' (Greatest Hits. AZL
    8601: Manilow Magic. ARTV 2)
'Riders To The Stars' (This One's For You. ARTY 137:
    Barry Manilow Live. DARTY 3)

S
'Sandra' (Barry Manilow II. ARTY 100)
'Say The Words' (This One's For You. ARTY 137)
'Seven More Years' (Barry Manilow. Bell 1129)
'She's A Star' (Tryin' To Get The Feeling. ARTY 123)
'Ships' (One Voice. SPART 1106)
'Sing It' (Barry Manilow. Bell 1129)
'Somethings Coming Up' (Barry Manilow II. ARTY 100)
'Somewhere In The Night' (Greatest Hits. AZL 8061: Even
    Now. SPART 1047)
'Starting Again' (Even Now. SPART 1047)
'Studio Musician' (Barry Manilow Live. DARTY 3)
'Sunday Father' (One Voice. SPART 1106)
'Sunrise' (Even Now. SPART 1047)
'Sweetwater Jones' (Barry Manilow. Bell 1129)
'Sweet Life' (Barry Manilow. Bell 1129)

T
'The Last Duet' (Barry. DART 2)
'The Two Of Us' (Barry Manilow II. ARTY 100)
'This One's For You' (This One's For You. ARTY 137:
    Greatest Hits. AZL 8601)
'Tryin' To Get The Feeling Again' (Tryin' To Get The
    Feeling. ARTY 123: Manilow Magic. ARTV 2)
'Twenty Four Hours A Day' (Barry. DART 2)

W

'We Still Have Time' (Barry.DARTY 2)

'Weekend In New England' (This One's For You. ARTY 137: Barry Manilow Live. DARTY 3: Greatest Hits. AZL 8061: Manilow Magic. ARTV 2)

'When I Wanted You' (One Voice. SPART 1106)

'Where Are They Now' (One Voice. SPART 1106)

'Where Do I Go From Here' (Even Now. SPART 1047)

'Who's Been Sleeping In My Bed' (One Voice. SPART 1106)

'Why Don't We Live Together' (Tryin' To Get The Feeling. ARTY 123: Barry Manilow Live. ARTY 3)

'Why Don't We See The Show Again' (This One's For You. ARTY 137)

Y

'You Could Show Me' (One Voice. SPART 1047)

'You're Leavin' Too Soon' (Tryin' To Get The Feeling. ARTY 123)

'You Oughta Be Home With Me' (This One's For You. ARTY 137.

SINGLES AND ALBUMS

Singles (UK):

1. 'Mandy'/'Something's Comin' Up' ARIST 001. February 1975 (11) 9
2. 'Tryin' To Get The Feeling'/'Nice Boy Like Me' ARIST 37
3. 'I Write The Songs'/'Sure As I'm Standing Here' ARIST 40. January 1976
4. 'Weekend In New England'/'Riders To The Stars' ARIST 77. October 1976
5. 'Looks Like We Made It'/'Weekend In New England'/'I Write The Songs' ARIST 120EP. July 1977
6. 'Daybreak'/'Jump Shout Boogie' ARIST 146. October 1977
7. 'Can't Smile Without You'/'Sunrise' ARIST 176. March 1978 (43) 7
8. 'Somewhere In The Night'/'Copacabana' ARIST 196. July 1978 (42) 10
9. 'Even Now'/'I Was A Fool' ARIST 220. October 1978
10. 'Could It Be Magic'/'I Am Your Child' ARIST 229. December 1978 (25) 10
11. 'Ready To Take A Chance Again'/'Sweet Life' ARIST 242. March 1979
12. 'I Write The Songs'/'As Sure As I'm Standing Here'

ARIST 280PD, re-issue with different catalogue number. May 1979

13. 'Ships'/'Sunday Father' ARIST 307. October 1979
14. 'Who's Been Sleeping In My Bed'/'They Gave In To The Blues' ARIST Barry 1. December 1979
15. 'It's A Miracle'/'I Don't Want To Walk Without You' ARIST 337. April 1980
16. 'Lonely Together'/'London' ARIST 373. November 1980 (21) 12
17. 'I Made It Through The Rain'/'Only In Chicago' ARIST 385. January 1981 (37) 6
18. 'Bermuda Triangle'/'One Voice' ARIST 406. March 1981 (15) 11
19. 'Let's Hang On' September 1981

Key: ARIST is for Arista record company. The number which follows is the record catalogue number. The figure in brackets is the highest chart position as recorded in the UK by the official industry/BBC chart compiled by the British Market Research Bureau for Music Week. The single/double figure which appears after the highest chart position is the number of weeks the record stayed in the UK, Top 75 singles listing.

Albums (UK): by title

1. Barry Manilow ARTY 100 January 1975 also titled Mandy
2. Tryin' To Get The Feeling ARTY 123 February 1976
3. This One's For You ARTY 137 October 1976
4. Live DARTY 3 October 1977
5. Even Now SPART 1047 April 1978
6. Manilow Magic ARTV 2 February 1979
7. One Voice SPART 1106 September 1979
8. Barry BARRY 2 November 1980
9. Box Set, three albums (Mandy, This One's For You,

Tryin' To Get The Feeling. (Limited edition.) BM BOX
1 December 1980

Import from US

1. Barry Manilow
2. Greatest Hits Double Album.

Albums (UK) Cassette. Release dates as for record.

1. Barry Manilow (also Mandy) TCART 100
2. Trying To Get The Feeling TCART 123
3. This One's For You TCART 137
4. Live TCDAR 3
5. Even Now TCART 1047
6. Manilow Magic ARTVC 2
7. One Voice TCART 1106
8. Barry TLART 2
9. Album Cassette Box TCBOX 1

AWARDS

1975

Record World, *Cashbox* (USA): Top new male vocalist, singles
and albums
Music Retailer: Top new male artist
Radio & Records: Pop Artist of the year

1976

Ruby Award – Performer of the year (USA)
Billboard and Cashbox: Top singles vocalist (USA)
American Guild of Variety Artists – Top vocalist

1977

American Music Award – Top vocalist
Photoplay Award: Favourite pop music star

BMI Award: Double award as composer of This One's For You and Daybreak (USA)

Tony Award: Engagement at Uris Theatre, New York (USA)

Emmy Award: Barry Manilow Special (US, TV)

1978

Seventeen Magazine (USA) Favourite male artist

BMI Award (USA) 'Mandy' for 1 million performances.

Billboard (USA) Top male album artist. Also, Top Easy Listening artist.

American Guild of Variety Artists: Top vocalist

Marketing and Music Award (USA) Advertisement jingles

Photoplay Gold Medal Awards (2) Favourite Variety Star.

Favourite B'Nia Brith Creative Achievement Award (USA)

American Music Award: Favourite male pop/rock vocalist

1979

Grammy Award – Best pop male vocalist for 'Copacabana'

American Favourite Music Award for male vocalist: pop/rock

Front Page Music Award: Top male vocalist: pop/rock

BMI Award for 'Even Now'/'Copacabana'. One million performances.

Canadian Disc Award: International male vocalist

1980

DJ Awards: Producer of the year for *Dionne* (the album which Barry produced for Dionne Warwick)

Music Week (UK) Award: Top selling album artist (Male)

1981

TV Times (UK): Most exciting male vocalist award.

Album Awards:

Barry Manilow is the only artist in the world ever to achieve three triple platinum albums within 18 months. The albums are *This One's For You* (7 January 1977), *Barry Manilow Live* (25 November 1977), *Even Now* (8 May 1978)
Barry Manilow I – Platinum
Barry Manilow II – Double Platinum
Tryin' To Get The Feeling – Double Platinum
This One's For You – Triple Platinum
Barry Manilow Live – Quadruple Platinum
Even Now – Triple Platinum
Barry Manilow – Greatest Hits (American version) – Triple Platinum

Manilow Magic went gold before UK release. Advanced orders for the LP saw it chart at the same time as the album *Even Now*.

Gold Singles:

'Mandy'. 'Looks Like We Made It'. 'Copacabana'. 'I Write The Songs'. 'Can't Smile Without You'.

(all from US sales)

Barry Manilow

8/8/80

Dear Mollie and Lynn —

In overwhelmed by your generous gift, grateful for all of your support, and very impressed with your newsletter.

In glad to hear that you're now working with Kate and the International Fan Club. Between you, Kate and Daryl in Australia, In sure my music will never die.

See you at Wembley!

love

Barry